PURNELL'S NEW

JUNIOR WORLD

ENCYCLOPEDIA

PURNELL'S NEW
JUNIOR WORLD
ENCYCLOPEDIA

Michael W. Dempsey B.A.

Purnell, London W.1.

Contributors

NEIL ARDLEY B.Sc.
A. L. BARRETT
N. S. BARRETT M.A.
CAROLE BERKSON
LUCY BERMAN B.A.
A. S. BUTTERFIELD
RONALD L. CARTER B.Sc.(ECON), F.R.G.S.
ANN CLARK
JOHN O. E. CLARK B.Sc., A.R.I.C.
J. N. CLEAVER M.A.
T. G.COOK M.A.
JEAN COOKE
JILL R. GIRLING B.A.
PETER GREY
R. J. W. HAMMOND
BRENDAN HENNESSY
L. JAMES M.A., PH.D.
ANN KRAMER
JO LOGAN
K. E. LOWTHER M.A.
KEITH LYE B.A., F.R.G.S.
L. H. MUNBY M.A.
DOMINIC RECALDIN B.Sc., PH.D.
THEODORE ROWLAND-ENTWISTLE F.R.G.S.
G.E. SATTERTHWAITE F.R.A.S.
D.S. SEHBAI M.A.
D. SHARP L.R.A.M.
G.M. WESTON B.A.
B. G. WILSON
MICHAEL E. WRIGHT B.A.

© 1969 B.P.C. Publishing Ltd.
Made and printed in Great Britain
by Purnell and Sons Ltd.
Paulton (Somerset) and London

Abacus An abacus is a frame of beads on wires, used for counting and for simple mathematical calculations. Its principle was known to the ancient Assyrians, and early Greeks and Romans used the bead-frame abacus. Today in Western countries it is used as a toy or to teach counting to young children. But in Eastern countries it is still used in shops, offices, and even in banks. The Chinese call it *suan pan* and the Japanese *soroban*.

Counting on an abacus is rather like counting on the fingers. For instance a simple frame may have rows of ten beads, each row from right to left standing for units, tens, hundreds, and so on. A modern Japanese abacus has only five beads instead of ten, each group of five being split into four and one by a bar across the frame. In the units 'column', the four beads count as 1, 2, 3 and 4 while the single bead counts as 5. It can be used for multiplying and dividing as well as for adding and subtracting.

the most important classes of chemical compounds. They are connected in the following way. An acid reacts with a base to give a salt and water. This is one of the fundamental rules in chemistry.

Hydrochloric acid, for example, combines with sodium hydroxide (base) to form sodium *chloride* (salt) and water. Sulphuric acid combines with potassium hydroxide (base) to form potassium *sulphate* (salt) and water. In a similar way nitric acid reacts to produce a *nitrate*. (See Alkalis; Salt.)

One way acids and bases differ is in their action towards a litmus solution. *Litmus* is one of the substances called *indicators,* which have one colour in an acid solution and another colour in an alkaline solution. In an acid solution, litmus is red; in an alkaline solution it is blue.

The three acids mentioned so far are inorganic compounds. There are also *organic* acids — those which contain car-

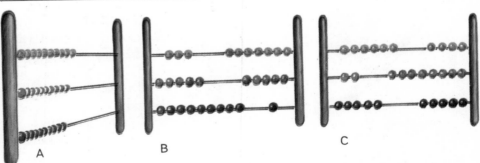

A simple abacus (A) has three rows of beads which count as one each, ten each, and one hundred each. In addition (B), beads are moved across from the left giving a total on the right. In subtraction (C), beads are taken away from the left leaving the remainder on the left.

A   B   C

Acids are a group of chemicals that are known for their sour taste. Some of the acids are very dangerous. *Sulphuric acid,* for example, is highly *corrosive* — it can eat away most metals. And it will quickly burn into flesh and other living matter. *Nitric acid* and *hydrochloric acid* are two other acids that will attack most metals. These three strong acids are among the most important of all the chemicals used in industry — sulphuric acid especially (see Sulphur).

Acids, bases and salts form three of

bon atoms. In general, organic acids are very much weaker than inorganic acids, and they are also very much more common. For example, vinegar is a weak solution of an organic acid called *acetic* acid. The sharp taste in citrus fruits such as lemons is caused by *citric* acid. When an ant stings us, it injects *formic* acid into the skin, which causes pain. *Lactic* acid causes the sourness when milk 'goes off'. Proteins, which living things need to build up tissue, are made up of *amino* acids.

2

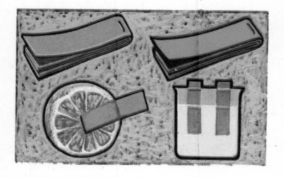

It is possible to tell whether a solution is acidic by testing it with blue litmus paper. Litmus is one of the substances called indicators. Any solution which changes the colour of litmus from blue to red is sure to contain some kind of acid. Red litmus paper (right) is unaffected by acids.

Most organic acids—those obtained from living things—are weak and generally harmless. In fact we eat them in the form of fruit and in vinegar.

Grapes Contain Tartaric Acid

Rhubarb Leaves Contain Oxalic Acid (Poison)   **Vinegar Contains Acetic Acid**

Unripe Apples and Pears Contain Malic Acid

Citrus Fruits, such as Oranges and Lemons, Contain Citric Acid

Acoustics In designing a concert hall or theatre, the architect must carefully consider the *acoustics* of the building. Will the full range of sound waves reach every seat in the auditorium? Will there be too much reflection, or is too much sound going to be absorbed by the walls and ceiling?

Sound waves travel in straight lines and will go out from their source in all directions. But in much the same way as with light, sound waves can be reflected or absorbed by surfaces which they strike.

The quality of the sound depends largely upon a portion of the sound waves reaching the listener by reflection. On the other hand, too many echoes are undesirable. Consequently, the height of the roof of the concert hall and the curvature of its surface have to be carefully chosen in order that the sound waves which it collects are reflected back so as to produce the most pleasing effect.

Various reflectors and baffles may be attached to the walls and ceiling to turn the sound waves in the most desirable direction. It is often necessary to have reflectors above the platform to throw the sound out into the body of the hall.

The presence of an audience has a considerable effect upon the acoustics of many concert halls, as the members of the audience are themselves quite good absorbers of sound waves. This particular problem can be overcome with tip-up seats so designed so that they have similar absorption properties to those of the audience who may occupy them.

Adelaide is the chief city and capital of the State of South Australia. It was founded in 1837 on the River Torrens, six miles inland from the shore of the St Vincent Gulf. A central position, ease of communications, and nearby mineral resources have contributed to its growth. With a population of 728,000 the city is

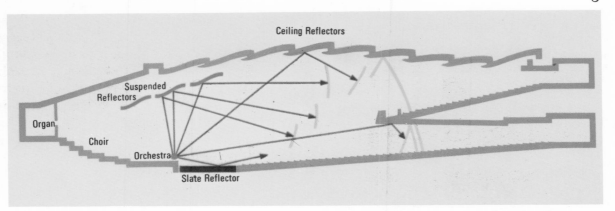

Ceiling Reflectors

Suspended
Reflectors

Organ

Choir

Orchestra

Slate Reflector

Modern auditoriums are carefully designed to have
good acoustic properties. Above: A section through a
concert hall showing where the sound waves are reflected.

Left: A modern concert hall based on this design.

an important centre of Australia's export
trade. Port Adelaide handles the bulk of
the produce of the surrounding fertile
plains, a rich wool, cereal and fruit
producing area. The city has fine public
buildings, two universities, cathedrals,
and an Institute of Technology.

Afghanistan is a land-locked Muslim
kingdom of southern Asia. Most Afghans
are farmers or craftsmen who live outside the few towns. Afghanistan is
bordered by Russia, China, Pakistan and
Iran.

Mountains cover nearly three-
quarters of Afghanistan. The snow-
capped Hindu Kush reaches 25,000 feet
above sea-level near Pakistan. Much
of the land is desert. Afghanistan has
about 12 inches of rainfall every year.
Temperatures vary from freezing point
in Kabul in January, to 120°F (49°C) in
the deserts of the south-west in July.

Only about one-fiftieth of Afghanistan's
land area—the fertile mountain valleys—
can be farmed. Miners work deposits of
several minerals, and the country has a
few small manufacturing industries.

Greek, Arab, Mongol and Persian
armies each occupied Afghanistan in
turn. Russia and Britain competed for
influence in Afghanistan in the 1800's,
and British armies from India fought
several frontier wars with Afghanistan.

After Pakistan became independent in
1947, Afghanistan disputed its frontiers.
Afghanistan claimed that *Pathan* tribes-
men, who live in both countries, should
be able to form their own state. The dispute continued into the late 1960's.

Facts and Figures
Area: 250,000 square miles.
Population: 15,960,000 (estimate).
Capital: Kabul.

Left: An Afghan girl in traditional dress.

Right: Location map of Afghanistan (black).

Below: The people of Afghanistan are noted for their fierce independence, and during the country's turbulent history they have gained a reputation as fearless fighters.

Africa is the world's second largest continent. With its area of 11,671,000 square miles, it is three and a half times as large as the United States. But Africa has only 320,000,000 people. The United States has about twice as many people to every square mile.

Large parts of Africa are almost empty wastelands. Great, burning-hot deserts, including the Sahara in the north and the Namib and Kalahari in the south, cover about two-fifths of Africa. Life is only possible where water is available. For example, nearly all Egyptians live in the valley of the River Nile. Either side of this valley is empty desert.

Near the Equator, especially in western and west-central Africa, the rainfall is very heavy, sometimes more than 150 inches a year. This hot, rain-drenched region is covered by thick, luxuriant forests. The trees grow so close together that their leaves blot out the sun.

Although most of Africa lies within the tropics, more than a third of the continent is a great *plateau* (high plain). Because they are so high, many parts of Africa close to the Equator have a pleasant climate. Travellers going inland from the steaming-hot seaports of Mombasa and Dar-es-Salaam in eastern Africa climb steeply to the plateau. Average temperatures fall at a rate of about 1° F for every 330 feet. In eastern Africa are the continent's two highest mountains, Kilimanjaro in Tanzania (19,340 feet above sea level) and Mount Kenya (17,058 feet) Snow and ice cap the peaks of these mountains.

Grassland called *savanna* covers much of the high plains of Africa. Great herds of animals still roam over Africa's grasslands and forests. In the past, thousands of animals were killed by hunters and poachers. To save the animals, many African governments have set up special parks and game reserves.

Throughout the eastern African plateau runs the deep African rift valley. This colossal valley stretches from Syria

Above: The Flamboyant tree, a native of southern Africa.

Right: The Negroes of eastern and southern Africa, such as the Masai and Zulus, have a lighter skin colour than the 'true' Negroes of western and central Africa.

Below: The Greater Kudu, one of the many species of antelope which roam the African plains.

in Asia through the Red Sea and eastern Africa to Mozambique. It contains many lakes, including Lake Tanganyika, the world's longest freshwater lake. The rift valley was formed when the ground sank between *faults*, or breaks, in the Earth's crust.

Africa's largest lake is Lake Victoria, which lies between Kenya and Tanzania. Africa's greatest rivers are the Nile, the Congo, the Niger and the Zambezi.

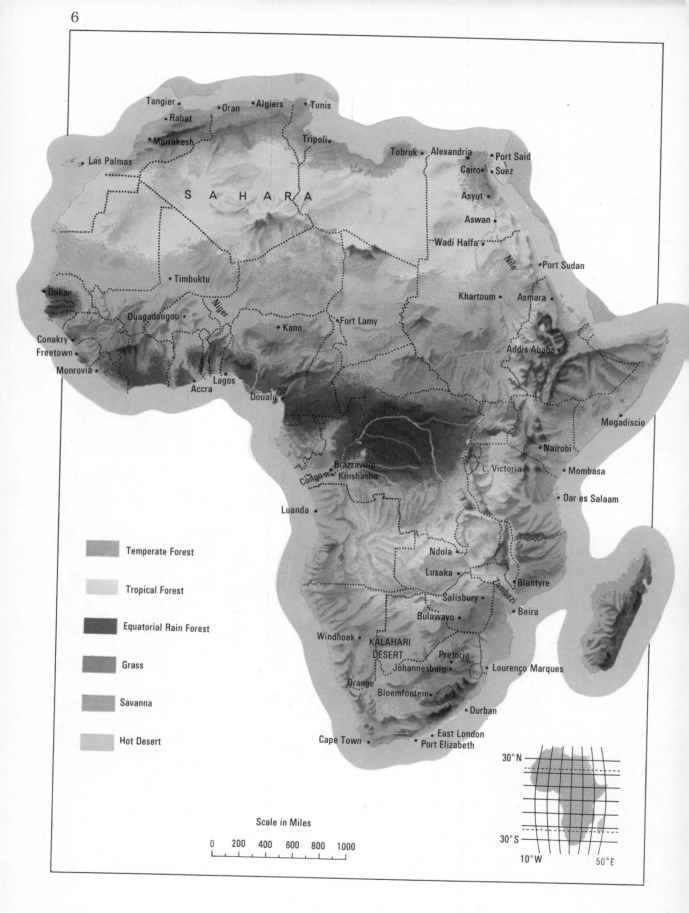

Tangier • Oran • Algiers • Tunis
• Rabat
Marrakesh • Tripoli •

• Las Palmas

S A H A R A

Tobruk • Alexandria
Cairo • Port Said
• Suez

Asyut •

Aswan •

Wadi Halfa •

Nile

• Port Sudan

• Timbuktu

Khartoum • Asmara •

Niger

Ouagadougou •

• Dakar

Fort Lamy •

• Kano

Conakry •
Freetown •

Addis Ababa •

Monrovia •

Accra
Lagos •

Douala •

Mogadiscio •

• Nairobi

Brazzaville
Congo • Kinshasha

L. Victoria

• Mombasa

• Dar es Salaam

Luanda •

Ndola •

Lusaka •
Zambezi
Salisbury •

Blantyre •

Bulawayo •

• Beira

Windhoek •

KALAHARI
DESERT

Pretoria •
Johannesburg •
Orange

• Lourenço Marques

Bloemfontein •

• Durban

Cape Town •

• East London
Port Elizabeth

Temperate Forest

Tropical Forest

Equatorial Rain Forest

Grass

Savanna

Hot Desert

Scale in Miles

0   200   400   600   800 1000

30° N

30° S

10° W   50° E

INDEPENDENT COUNTRIES OF AFRICA

Country	Area (sq. mi.)	Population	Capital
Algeria	919,800	12,000,000	Algiers
Botswana	222,000	576,000	Gaberones
Burundi	10,747	3,000,000	Bujumbura
Cameroon	183,569	5,550,000	Yaoundé
Central African Rep.	236,294	2,900,000	Bangui
Chad	495,754	3,400,000	Fort-Lamy
Congo (Brazzaville)	132,047	864,000	Brazzaville
Congo (Kinshasa)	905,565	15,700,000	Kinshasa
Dahomey	43,483	2,400,000	Porto-Novo
Egypt (U.A.R.)	386,101	31,150,000	Cairo
Equatorial Guinea	10,832	245,000	Santa Isabel
Ethiopia	457,267	22,350,000	Addis Ababa
Gabon	103,089	470,000	Libreville
Gambia	4,003	330,000	Bathurst
Ghana	92,100	8,164,000	Accra
Guinea	94,926	3,500,000	Conakry
Ivory Coast	124,503	4,100,000	Abidjan
Kenya	224,960	9,104,000	Nairobi
Lesotho	11,716	1,000,000	Maseru
Liberia	43,000	1,066,000	Monrovia
Libya	679,360	1,617,000	Bengasi; Tripoli
Madagascar (Malagasy Rep.)	230,035	6,751,000	Tananarive
Malawi	46,066	4,042,000	Zomba
Mali	463,949	4,900,000	Bamako
Mauritania	419,230	900,000	Nouakchott
Mauritius	809	803,000	Port Louis
Morocco	172,413	14,300,000	Rabat; Tangier
Niger	489,190	4,034,000	Niamey
Nigeria	356,669	60,500,000	Lagos
Rwanda	10,169	3,018,000	Kigali
Senegal	75,750	3,580,000	Dakar
Sierra Leone	27,699	2,183,000	Freetown
Somalia	246,202	2,500,000	Mogadiscio
South Africa	471,466	18,700,000	Cape Town; Pretoria
Sudan	967,501	13,540,000	Khartoum
Swaziland	6,704	389,000	Mbabane
Tanzania	362,820	12,231,000	Dar es Salaam
Togo	21,853	1,800,000	Lomé
Tunisia	48,332	4,675,000	Tunis
Uganda	91,134	7,740,000	Kampala
Upper Volta	105,869	4,882,000	Ouagadougou
Zambia	288,130	3,894,000	Lusaka

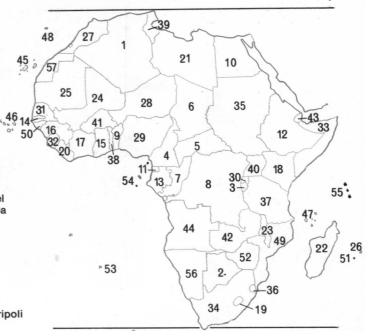

Key to Independent Countries

1, Algeria; 2, Botswana; 3, Burundi; 4, Cameroon; 5, Central African Republic; 6, Chad; 7, Congo (Brazzaville); 8, Congo (Kinshasa); 9, Dahomey; 10, Egypt; 11, Equatorial Guinea; 12, Ethiopia; 13, Gabon; 14, Gambia; 15, Ghana; 16, Guinea; 17, Ivory Coast; 18, Kenya; 19, Lesotho; 20, Liberia; 21, Libya; 22, Madagascar (Malagasy Republic); 23, Malawi; 24, Mali; 25, Mauritania; 26, Mauritius; 27, Morocco; 28, Niger; 29, Nigeria; 30, Rwanda; 31, Senegal; 32, Sierra Leone; 33, Somalia; 34, South Africa; 35, Sudan; 36, Swaziland; 37, Tanzania; 38, Togo; 39, Tunisia; 40, Uganda; 41, Upper Volta; 42, Zambia.

Key to Colonies and Territories

43, Afars and Issas; 44, Angola; 45, Canary Islands; 46, Cape Verde Islands; 47, Comoro Islands; 48, Madeira Islands; 49, Mozambique; 50, Portuguese Guinea; 51, Réunion; 52, Rhodesia; 53, St. Helena; 54, São Tomé and Principe; 55, Seychelles Islands; 56, South West Africa; 57, Spanish Sahara.

AFRICAN COLONIES AND TERRITORIES

Name	Area (sq. mi.)	Population	Capital	Status
Afars and Issas	8,494	81,000	Djibouti	French colony
Angola	481,352	4,830,000	Luanda	Portuguese province
Canary Islands	2.808	908,718	Santa Cruz de Tenerife; Las Palmas	Spanish province
Cape Verde Islands	1,557	202,000	Praia	Portuguese province
Comoro Islands	838	177,000	Dzaoudzi	French colony
Madeira Islands	308	269,769	Funchal	Portuguese district
Mozambique	302,329	6,529,000	Lourenço Marques	Portuguese province
Portuguese Guinea	13,948	519,000	Bissau	Portuguese province
Réunion	969	397,000	Saint Denis	French department
Rhodesia	150,333	4,500,000	Salisbury	British colony*
Saint Helena	47	4,702	Jamestown	British colony
São Tomé & Príncipe	372	63,000	São Tomé	Portuguese province
Seychelles Islands	156	48,700	Victoria	British colony
South West Africa	318,261	610,000	Windhoek	South African mandate
Spanish Sahara	102,703	36,000	Aiún	Spanish province

* Rhodesia declared its independence in 1965, but Britain did not recognize this act.

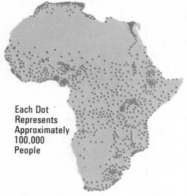

Each Dot Represents Approximately 100,000 People

Above: Population distribution map of Africa.
Right: The lowlands of equatorial Africa are covered with dense forests which contain many valuable hardwoods.

North of the Sahara, most of the people are Arabs or Berbers. They follow the Muslim religion. Negroid Africans, who make up three-quarters of Africa's population, live south of the Sahara. Some of them follow tribal religions. More than five million people of European ancestry live in Africa, many of them in South Africa. Their ancestors were the pioneers who introduced western ideas of farming, mining and industry. About half a million people of Asian origin also live in Africa. About 35,000,000 people, including most of the Europeans, are Christians.

Most Africans are farmers. They either rear cattle or grow crops to feed their families. The wealth of many African countries is based on one or two crops which are grown on plantations. For example, Ghana's most important export is cocoa. Eastern Africa's main products are coffee and sisal. Africa produces nearly three-quarters of the world's palm oil and palm kernels. Other crops include cotton, fruits, tea and tobacco.

Africa produces almost all the world's diamonds and a large quantity of gold. Other important minerals are copper, cobalt, petroleum and uranium. Africa has

Right: In 1875 European interests in Africa were confined mainly to coastal settlements. But the following 25 years saw the 'scramble for Africa', with the European powers carving up the continent between them. These undeveloped lands provided a new market for the products of Europe's factories. Since the Second World War most of these former colonies have gained their independence.

1875

Territories under European Control

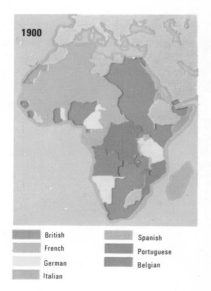

1900

British
French
German
Italian

Spanish
Portuguese
Belgian

little coal, but hydro-electric power is used by the few manufacturing industries.

Northern Africa was important in the early growth of civilizations around the Mediterranean Sea. The Nile valley was the centre of one of the greatest early civilizations. (See Egypt, Ancient.)

But little was known of Africa south of the Sahara. Arab traders visited the area and found great empires in western Africa. But to Europeans, Africa was a 'dark' continent. After Vasco da Gama had sailed to Asia around the southern tip of Africa in 1497, many ships used this route. Soon the African coastline was charted. But few people were interested in exploring the interior.

From the 1400's, European sailors began to ship slaves from Africa. The slave trade continued until the 1800's. An estimated 14 million African slaves were

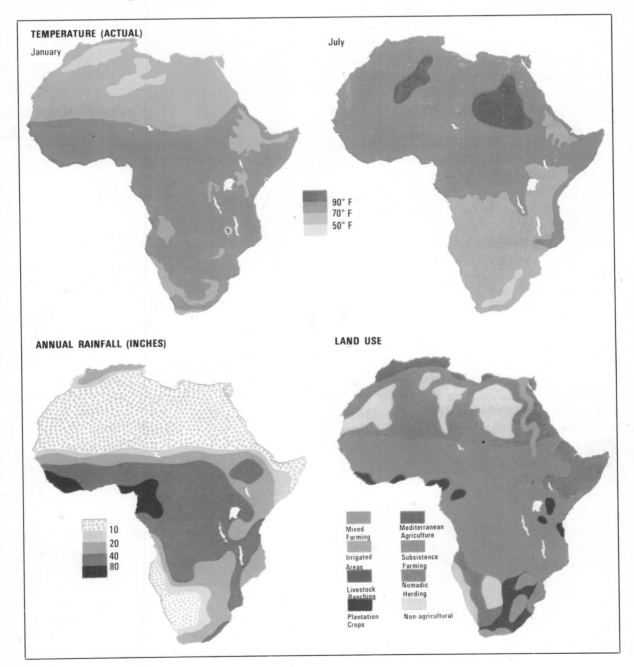

TEMPERATURE (ACTUAL)

January

July

90° F
70° F
50° F

ANNUAL RAINFALL (INCHES)

10
20
40
80

LAND USE

Mixed Farming

Mediterranean Agriculture

Irrigated Areas

Subsistence Farming

Livestock Ranching

Nomadic Herding

Plantation Crops

Non-agricultural

10

shipped to the Americas. Usually the slave traders bought slaves from African coastal chiefs whose people raided inland tribes. European traders seldom travelled inland.

An early and important settlement at the Cape of Good Hope was established in 1652. This settlement developed to form part of present-day South Africa.

The great period of European exploration of the interior came during the 1800's. Many explorers were missionaries who helped to stamp out the terrible slave trade. Bold men, such as David Livingstone in southern Africa, Mungo Park in western Africa and Henry Morton Stanley in the Congo region, braved many hardships to discover the secrets of Africa. (See Exploration.)

Information brought back by explorers interested European governments, who began to establish settlements and colonies. By the 1890's, almost all of Africa was divided up between the European powers.

From the 1890's to the 1950's, most African countries were European colonies. The Europeans introduced new ways of life and developed Africa. But many Africans resented foreign rule. In the late 1950's and early 1960's, nearly all African countries achieved independence.

Most of the countries are poor. Partly as a result of their poverty, many countries were unsettled during the 1960's. Army leaders overthrew several elected governments. Some countries adopted one-party rule. In Congo (Kinshasa) and in Nigeria, terrible civil wars led to many deaths and much suffering.

Ageing When animals grow old, noticeable changes take place in their appearance and the way they function. For instance, in man the skin becomes wrinkled and the hair grey. A person's memory becomes poor and he cannot use his limbs so well. This happens in all *warm-blooded* animals and birds. They lose their vigour

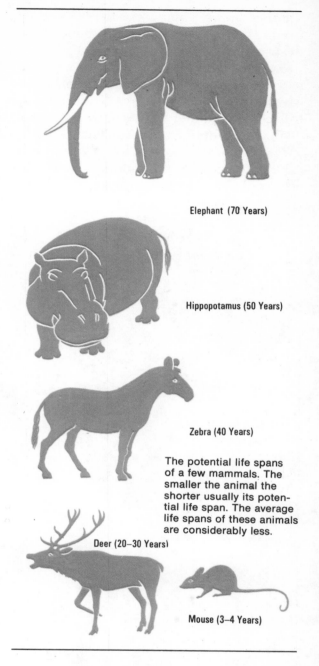

Elephant (70 Years)

Hippopotamus (50 Years)

Zebra (40 Years)

The potential life spans of a few mammals. The smaller the animal the shorter usually its potential life span. The average life spans of these animals are considerably less.

Deer (20–30 Years)

Mouse (3–4 Years)

and *adaptability*.

As they get older, most creatures are less able to adapt themselves to changes and influences in their surroundings. They are no longer able to cope with certain unfavourable conditions, so that they become more prone to diseases and disabilities, particularly to the effects of non-infectious diseases. Excessive cold and damp, or too little food, leave an old animal more vulnerable than a younger one. At the same time, as these effects take place, the creature can take less exercise.

Among the mammals there seems to be some link between size and *life span* (length of life). Smaller animals age more quickly. Elephants are known to live for up to 70 years, horses up to 40 years, cows 30 years, dogs 20 years, mice only about 4 years. These are maximum ages. Even more important seems to be brain size. Man, who has — in relation to body size — the biggest brain of all mammals, commonly outlives the elephant.

Birds generally have even longer natural life spans than mammals of equal size. Parrots and eagles, for instance, can probably live for over 100 years. Cold-blooded amphibians and reptiles live even longer, in relation to size. Frogs and toads can pass the age of 20, while giant tortoises may live nearly 200 years.

Air is the mixture of gases that we breathe. It surrounds the Earth to a height of about 300 miles. It is often called the *atmosphere*. Nearly four-fifths of the air is made up of nitrogen (78%) and more than a fifth is oxygen (21%). Most of the remainder is argon (0·9%). There are small amounts of many other gases in the air, including hydrogen, helium, neon, and carbon dioxide.

Aircraft Man has long envied birds for their ability to fly freely through the air. At first, men tried to fly by attaching artificial wings to their arms and flapping them. But their muscles were not strong enough for the task.

It was the English scientist Sir George Cayley who first proposed in the early 1800's that a flying machine should be designed as a bird with fixed wings.

In 1903, two American brothers, Wilbur and Orville Wright, built a flimsy machine of wood, cloth and wire which was powered by a petrol engine. On December 17, Orville made the first powered flight on a deserted beach at Kitty Hawk, North Carolina.

After the Wrights had given demonstrations in Europe in 1908, aircraft development was rapid. In 1909, Louis Bleriot flew the English Channel. Aircraft were used widely in the First World War (1914-18), first for reconnaissance and then for fighting. Machine-guns were mounted in the nose, and bombs were dropped by hand. Most aircraft were biplanes — they had two wings, one above the other.

In 1919, John Alcock and Arthur Whitten-Brown made the first Atlantic crossing in a converted Vickers *Vimy* bomber. Charles Lindbergh made the first solo crossing in *Spirit of St. Louis* in 1927.

By the 1930's, aircraft were made of metal rather than of wood and fabric. They were streamlined, with retractable undercarriages, and had enclosed cabins. In 1936, the most successful commercial aircraft ever built — the Douglas DC-3, or Dakota — went into service.

High-speed fighter aircraft such as the Spitfire and heavy bombers such as the Flying Fortress played a vital role in the Second World War (1939-45). By the end of the war, both the Germans and the British had developed jet aircraft. In 1947, a rocket-powered aircraft, the American Bell XS-1, flew faster than the speed of sound. In 1952, the first jet airliner — the British Comet — went into regular service. Today, fighter aircraft which travel at more than twice the speed of sound serve in the world's air forces. Some airliners, too, are designed for such supersonic speeds.

To be able to fly, an aircraft must in some way lift itself off the ground against the Earth's gravity. This lift is produced by the movement of air over the aircraft's wings. The wings have a special cross-sectional shape, called an *aerofoil*, to produce lift. The aerofoil is sharply curved at the top and fairly flat at the bottom.

Air passing over the top surface travels faster than the air beneath because it

One of the great pioneers of heavier-than-air flight was the German engineer Otto Lilienthal who made more than 2,000 successful glider flights. His first glider was built of canvas, willow and bamboo, braced with strong wires, and he took off by running down a slope. Most of Lilienthal's gliders were monoplanes, but one was a biplane. He controlled them by swinging his legs and shifting the weight of his body. Lilienthal was killed while flying a glider in 1896. Seven years later the Wright brothers made the first powered flight in a heavier-than-air machine. Since that historic moment there has been a rapid development in aircraft design, and the advent of the jet-liner has revolutionised long-distance travel.

The Cavalcade of Flight

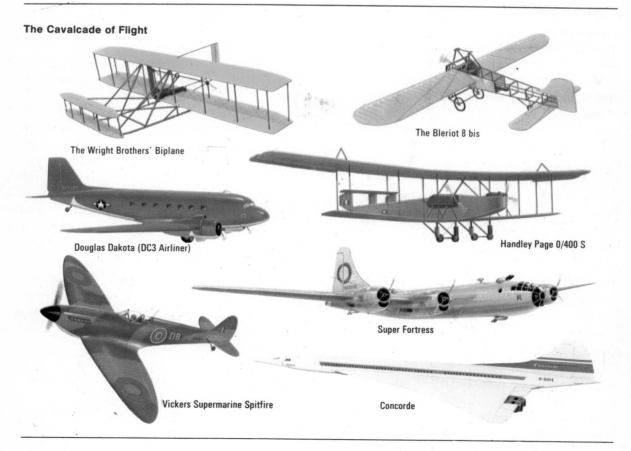

The Wright Brothers' Biplane

The Bleriot 8 bis

Douglas Dakota (DC3 Airliner)

Handley Page 0/400 S

Vickers Supermarine Spitfire

Super Fortress

Concorde

has farther to go. This means that the air pressure above the wing is less than that below it. The suction produced in this way lifts the wing. The lift is increased by angling the wing upwards slightly. This angle is called the angle of incidence.

The *thrust,* or force, needed to push the aircraft forward through the air comes either from a propeller or from a jet engine. Propeller blades have an aerofoil shape, too, and the suction created 'pulls' the propeller along. In a jet, the thrust comes from the *reaction* to hot gases rushing backwards from the engine. The hot gases exert a tremendous pressure on the front (closed) ends of the combustion chambers in the engine, but no pressure on the rear (open) ends where they are free to escape. It is this difference in pressure which produces the forward thrust.

This thrust is always opposed by the resistance, or *drag,* of the air on the aircraft body. Drag is reduced by building a smooth, streamlined body. For high-speed flight the wings are swept back from the body to reduce drag.

Most aircraft today are powered by jet engines. But some are still driven by propellers powered by piston engines using petrol. These engines work in much the same way as automobile engines but have different cylinder arrangements and may be air-cooled.

Jet engines produce much more power than piston engines of the same weight. They use a cheaper fuel (kerosene), too, but burn it at an enormous rate — 1,000 gallons an hour or more. The most widely used jet engine is the *turbo-jet.* Air is sucked in and compressed by a special kind of fan called a *compressor.* The compressed air is then forced into combustion chambers where it is mixed with fuel and burned. The hot gases produced escape at high speed from the engine's exhaust to produce thrust. Before the gases escape, they spin the blades on a turbine which drives the compressor. For this reason,

this engine is called a *gas turbine.*

The *turbo-prop* is similar in general design to the turbo-jet, but most of the thrust comes from a propeller driven by the turbine.

The latest engines have two sets of compressors driven by two separate turbines. They are called *two-spool* engines. The *by-pass turbojet* engine is similar to the two-spool type but some of the air from the front compressor goes directly to the exhaust and makes the engine more efficient.

The *ram-jet* is the simplest jet of all, but works only at high speeds. It is basically a long tube through which air is forced. Fuel is sprayed into the air stream and burned.

The *pulse-jet* is similar, but it has valves which close the air intake while the fuel is burned. Burning is therefore not continuous but in 'pulses'. This was the engine used in the V-1 missiles used by the Germans to bomb London in the Second World War.

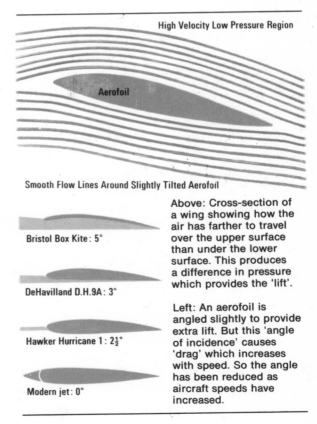

High Velocity Low Pressure Region

Aerofoil

Smooth Flow Lines Around Slightly Tilted Aerofoil

Bristol Box Kite: 5°

DeHavilland D.H.9A: 3°

Hawker Hurricane 1: 2½°

Modern jet: 0°

Above: Cross-section of a wing showing how the air has farther to travel over the upper surface than under the lower surface. This produces a difference in pressure which provides the 'lift'.

Left: An aerofoil is angled slightly to provide extra lift. But this 'angle of incidence' causes 'drag' which increases with speed. So the angle has been reduced as aircraft speeds have increased.

14

The main part of the aircraft body is the fuselage. At the front end is the cockpit, which houses the instruments and controls for the aircraft. Behind is the passenger cabin. In most aircraft, the fuselage is pressurized to make up for the decrease in air pressure when flying at high altitudes (30-40,000 feet).

The wings are attached to the fuselage. Sections of the trailing (rear) edges of the wings, called *ailerons*, are hinged. They can be moved up and down to cause the aircraft to tilt, or *bank*. Next to the ailerons are movable sections called *flaps*, which help to increase lift at low speeds and also act as air brakes.

At the rear of the aircraft is the tail, which steadies the craft and helps to control its flight. Moving a rudder at the rear of the upright tail fin turns the aircraft to the left or right. Moving elevators at the rear of the horizontal tail plane control the up-and-down movement of the aircraft.

The pilot controls the aircraft from the cockpit. He has a steering wheel or column which he moves back and forth to control the elevators or from side to side to control the ailerons. He controls the rudder by foot pedals.

A wide variety of dials and warning lights in the cockpit keep the pilot informed about how the various systems in the aircraft are working, whether he is on course, and so on. The main flight instruments are an altimeter to show the altitude, an air-speed indicator, and a compass to indicate direction.

There are a variety of instruments for navigation, too. An automatic pilot keeps the aircraft on course when the pilot leaves the controls. The aircraft may also carry radar and other electronic equipment for making 'blind' landings.

Planning, designing and testing a new aircraft takes many years. Designers test scale models of their aircraft in wind tunnels to find out how their aircraft will behave in real flight. They generally build full-size models, or 'mock-ups' of

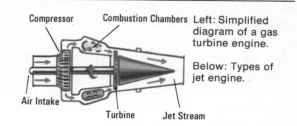

Left: Simplified diagram of a gas turbine engine.

Below: Types of jet engine.

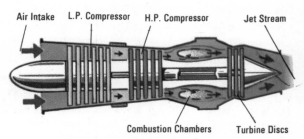

Two-spool or Supercharged Turbojet Engine

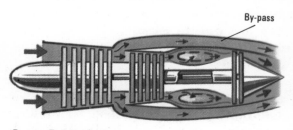

By-pass Turbojet Engine

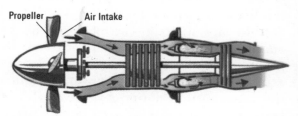

Turboprop Engine

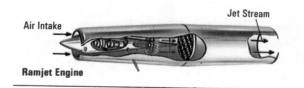

Ramjet Engine

wood to help them in detailed design and layout.

Engineers test full-size parts of the aircraft on test rigs or in pressure tanks under conditions similar to those found in flight to see whether the parts are strong enough. Many of the parts are twisted and stressed until they break. One of the great problems to overcome is *metal fatigue*, which may occur after prolonged stress and vibration.

The first aircraft built, called a prototype, is tested thoroughly on the ground and in flight before production begins.

Light alloys are used for the metal skeleton of ribs and spars that form the framework of the aircraft. The surface skin over the skeleton is made up of thin alloy sheets riveted together. Aluminium alloys are widely used in aircraft construction because of their lightness.

Airport A large modern airport is a scene of intense activity both by day and by night. At peak periods, huge jet airliners, weighing over 200 tons and carrying 150 or more passengers, take off or land every minute or so. More than 150 million passengers fly every year.

To deal with such vast amounts of traffic, every activity must be carefully co-ordinated. As soon as an aircraft has landed on the runway, it moves along a taxiway to an area called an *apron*. Immediately, trucks to carry baggage and buses to carry passengers hurry towards it. Then fuel tankers move in to refill the airliner's fuel tanks. A quick turn-around is always aimed for because the airliner is not earning any money while it is on the ground.

The most important people at the airport are the air-traffic controllers in the control tower, who supervise the landing and take-off of each aircraft. They bring down an aircraft from a height of five or six miles onto a runway about two miles long and 200 feet wide. Most airports have a criss-cross pattern of main runways so that aircraft can always land against the wind, which is much safer.

Aircraft contact the control tower as they approach the airport. If the runways are full, the controller tells the aircraft to circle one above the other until the runway is free. This is called *stacking*.

The ground controller uses a variety of instruments to bring the aircraft down safely in all kinds of weather. His main

Upper picture: The cockpit of a modern airliner, showing the maze of instruments and controls.
Lower picture: DC-9 jet aircraft on the production line.

ones are radio and radar. His radar screen indicates the direction and distance of the aircraft. He can therefore guide the aircraft in by radio contact.

Other electronic devices aid landing. The Instrument Landing System puts aircraft on the right flight path. The Automatic Landing System guides and lands the aircraft automatically.

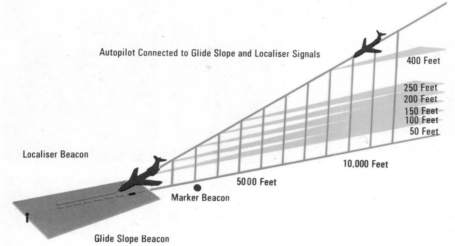

Autopilot Connected to Glide Slope and Localiser Signals

400 Feet

250 Feet
200 Feet
150 Feet
100 Feet
50 Feet

Localiser Beacon

10,000 Feet

5000 Feet

Marker Beacon

Glide Slope Beacon

Top left: Aircraft arriving at a busy airport may have to queue in 'stacks' at different levels awaiting their turn to land. When the runway is clear, the aircraft at the bottom of the stack is allowed to land and the rest move down one level.

Bottom left: In a blind-landing system an aircraft is automatically guided down onto the runway by a mechanical 'autopilot'. A localiser beacon tells the autopilot where the runway centre line is; a guide-slope beacon marks the correctly angled approach path; and a marker indicates the distance to the runway threshold.

Below: trapping for furs is still an important activity in Alaska.

Alaska is the most northerly state of the United States. It is also the largest, with an area of 586,400 square miles. The Americans bought it from the Russians in 1867 for £7,200,000.

About one-third of Alaska lies north of the Arctic Circle. Snow and ice cover the land for much of the year. The people who live in this area include Eskimos, short, stocky people who live by hunting seals, fish and reindeer. Polar bears also roam northern Alaska.

The central and inland parts of Alaska contain a horseshoe-shaped range of mountains, high plains and thick forests. The 1,800-mile Yukon River flows through this region.

Running down the Pacific coast is a narrow strip of land known as the Panhandle. It has many *fjords*, steep-sided sea inlets, and thick forests. Its climate is mild, with plenty of rain.

Besides Eskimos, American Indians and Aleuts—people similar to the Eskimos—

live in Alaska. But most of the 248,000 people are of European origin, living in Anchorage, the largest city, Juneau, the capital, and other cities.

Alaska has a number of growing industries, but fishing, especially for salmon, is still the chief one. Its mines produce coal and various metals, such as gold and platinum, while petroleum and natural gas have now been found there. Fur-trapping and lumbering are also important.

Left: Location map of Albania (marked in black), showing its position in relation to Italy.

Facts and Figures
Area: 11,000 square miles.
Population: 1,919,000.
Capital: Tirana.

Left: Location map of Alaska (marked in black), showing its position in North America.

The explorers Aleksandr Chirikov and Vitus Bering first reached Alaska from Russia in 1741, and the first permanent settlement was made by Russians on Kodiak Island in 1784. But the area was not developed much until 1899 when gold was discovered there. Though the 'gold rush' days have long since passed, Alaska has continued to develop. During World War II it became a vital defence base.

Albania is a small, mountainous country in south-eastern Europe. It lies on the Adriatic Sea. Greece borders Albania to the south-east and Yugoslavia to the north and east. The Albanian Alps, which cover most of the country, make communications difficult.

Most Albanians live on farms or in isolated mountain villages. They are mainly Muslims, but some are Christians. Those on the coast fish. The farmers grow wheat, tobacco, maize and cotton, and raise cattle, sheep, pigs and goats. Albania's few industries include food processing and cloth making. Albania has large mineral deposits and petroleum is exported.

Albania was part of the Turkish Empire for 400 years and became independent in 1912. It has been a communist state since 1945 and now receives political and economic aid from communist China.

Albatross The albatross is a member of the petrel family. Petrels are also called *tube-noses,* because their nostrils open through tubes on top of the beak.

The albatross is an oceanic bird that often stays far out to sea for months on end. It is a wonderful flier. It soars easily over the waves, and comes ashore only to breed, or when driven there by storms. The wandering albatross has a wing span of 11 feet, the largest span of any living bird. There are 13 species of albatrosses and most of them live in the far south of the southern hemisphere.

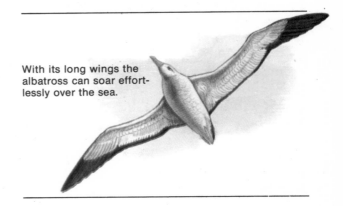

With its long wings the albatross can soar effortlessly over the sea.

A painting by Joseph Wright (1771) shows the German alchemist Hennig Brand praying after his discovery in 1669 of a new element. His laboratory is lighted by the glow of his discovery—phosphorus.

Alchemy We know today that every substance is made up of a number of chemical elements in combination. Each element is different from every other element. And one element cannot be changed into another by normal chemical means. This picture of matter began slowly to emerge during the 1600's and 1700's.

Before then, most people believed that there were only four basic 'elements'—fire, air, water, and earth. The great Greek philosopher Aristotle first put forward this view in the 300's B.C. Every substance was believed to be made up of a different combination of these four elements. But the proportion of the elements could be altered by adding some of the other elements, which meant that every substance could be changed into any other substance.

This led to a quest for methods of changing lead and other so-called 'base' metals into gold. People began to believe that there was a magical substance called the *philosopher's stone,* or *elixir,* which had the power to carry out this change.

The people who carried out experiments to make the philosopher's stone, with a mixture of science and magic, were called *alchemists.* They also considered that the philosopher's stone, or elixir, had the power to make human beings immortal. Small wonder then that alchemy was widely practised and attracted royalty, scholars and rogues alike. It became closely associated with astrology because of a belief that metals were linked with the heavenly bodies.

Of course, the alchemists had no luck in their quest. But it is from their methods, apparatus, observations, and accidental discoveries that the modern science of chemistry developed.

Alcohol If a person drinks too much beer or wine he becomes *intoxicated.* The intoxicating substance in these drinks is alcohol. It is formed by a process called *fermentation,* in which tiny organisms called *yeasts* act on natural sugars.

Wine, for example, is made from juice pressed from grapes. Yeasts from the grapes get into the juice and feed on the sugar it contains to produce alcohol and carbon dioxide gas, which bubbles off. Cider is made from apples in a similar way. Beer is produced by fermenting grain, usually barley.

When the alcohol reaches a certain level it kills the yeast and prevents further fermentation. To increase the amount of alcohol, the fermented liquid must be *distilled.* The alcohol boils away first and is condensed (turned back into liquid). The so-called 'spirits', such as whisky, brandy and gin are distilled.

Industrially, alcohol is often made from cereals and potatoes. It is widely used as a *solvent,* or dissolving substance, for many organic chemicals. It is used as such in lacquers.

Alcohol is one of a group of chemicals called the alcohols. It is also called *ethanol* and *ethyl alcohol.* Other im-

Malt whisky is made from barley which is allowed to germinate then roasted above a peat fire and mashed with water. Yeast is added and the fermenting liquid is distilled in pear-shaped copper-stills. The alcohol vapour is led through water-cooled pipes where it condenses to liquid whisky.

portant alcohols include *methanol,* or *wood alcohol,* used in methylated spirits. *Ethylene glycol* is another alcohol, used for antifreeze.

Alexander the Great (356-323 B.C.) was a powerful ruler and a brilliant military leader. He conquered much of the civilized world, spreading Greek culture throughout his territories.

As a boy, Alexander was tutored by Aristotle, who taught him to love Greek literature and philosophy. He became king of Macedonia before he was 20, when his father was assassinated. The Greek states were restless under Macedonian rule, and began to revolt against the young king. Alexander stormed the city of Thebes, destroying nearly every build-

ing. The spirit of the rebellion was broken, and the Greek states joined together under Alexander.

Having united Greece, Alexander launched a war on Persia. With 30,000 foot soldiers and 5,000 cavalry, he marched into Syria. Two years later it was his. He continued his march into Egypt. Weary of Persian rule, the Egyptians welcomed his coming. He founded the great city of Alexandria in Egypt. He defeated Darius, the Persian king, in the historical battle of

Bust of Alexander the Great.

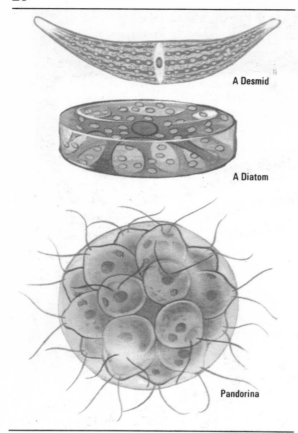

A Desmid

A Diatom

Pandorina

Algae range in size from microscopic single-celled forms to brown seaweeds 50 yards long.

Top left: A desmid and a diatom, two single-celled microscopic algae.

Bottom left: Pandorina, a microscopic colonial algae which consists of 16 identical cells arranged in a solid ball embedded in jelly. Each cell acts as an individual plant.

Top right: A leaf-like red seaweed.

Bottom right: A common brown seaweed.

Far right: Bladder wrack with a diagram showing the reproductive pits (conceptacles). Male and female cells are released from them and join together in the water to form new plants.

Red Seaweed

Channelled Wrack

Arbela. Babylon, Susa, and Persepolis, the richest and most beautiful cities of the time, opened their gates to welcome his coming.

Alexander died at Babylon, which he had made capital of his vast empire. At the height of his power, this empire reached from Greece to north-western India.

Algae are plants that grow in water or in damp places. The ones that grow on the sea-shore are called seaweeds. A visit to the sea-side tells you how numerous ocean forms are, while fresh-water forms often give rise to the green scum on ponds you see in the summer. Terrestrial forms—those that do not live in water— are not so common, but you may see one form growing as a green crusty coating on tree trunks—particularly on the tree's shaded side.

Algae contain some of the largest as well as the smallest kinds of life. In this enormous group of plants—about 17,000 species are known to man—many kinds consist of just one cell and can be seen only with a microscope. But certain brown seaweeds, called *kelps,* grow more than 50 yards long. Some single-celled forms are more like animals than plants, since they can move about. They have *flagella*—long hair-like out-growths of the body—that drive the organism through the water with whip-like lashing movements. Between single-celled forms and large seaweeds are several *colonial* algae, where groups of cells, each retaining a more or less separate way of life, combine and move about as one.

Algae are a vital link in the chain of life in the water. Single-celled forms, such as desmids and diatoms, make up floating 'soups' of microscopic organisms collectively called *plankton*. Plankton is a basic source of food for all animal life in the water, both in the sea and in fresh water.

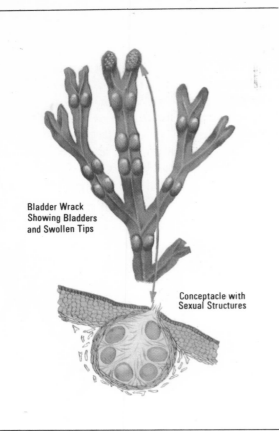

Bladder Wrack Showing Bladders and Swollen Tips

Conceptacle with Sexual Structures

Algae do possess the green pigment chlorophyll, the substance that traps light energy and puts it to work to make sugars. A lot of algae do not look green, but this is because they contain other pigments besides chlorophyll, which mask the green colour.

Algeria is the second largest country in Africa. Situated in the north-west, its coastline faces the Mediterranean Sea. Most Algerians are Arabs or Berbers who live in the most fertile northern part

Location map of Algeria (marked in black), showing its position in Africa.

Facts and Figures
Area: 919,800 square miles.
Population: 12,000,000.
Capital: Algiers.

Seaweeds provide protection for animal life by the sea-shore. Most seaweeds are covered in a slimy substance, called *mucilage,* which prevents them losing water and, at the same time, produces a conveniently moist shelter for marine animals when the tide goes out.

From a botanical point of view, algae are rather primitive. If you compare them with flowering plants, for example, you find that algae have no proper stems, leaves, or roots, though certain seaweeds have a root-like structure known as a *holdfast.*

Algae do not have flowers. Instead of the pollen and egg cells of flowering plants, most algae release male and female sex cells of fairly similar size and shape into the water. Nearly all algae can also reproduce without sex cells. The contents of a cell divide into a number of 'units', and the cell then bursts open. Each 'unit' released is capable of developing into a new plant.

of the country. The centre and south is part of the waterless Sahara. The Atlas Mountains separate the fertile coastlands from the sun-baked desert.

Temperatures in the north sometimes reach 100° F (38° C) in summer. But they fall below freezing point in winter. Between 18 and 30 inches of rain fall every year in the north.

Less than a quarter of all Algerians live in towns or cities. Most of the others are farmers. Important exports include fruit, iron ore, phosphates and wine. Today petroleum and natural gas extracted from under the Sahara are also becoming important. The gas and oil are piped northwards to the coast and then shipped to Europe.

In the A.D. 600's, Arabs occupied Algeria, and in the 1500's it became part of the Turkish Empire. From 1830, many French people settled in Algeria, which became a province of France. Algeria won its independence in 1962.

Alkalis Caustic soda and caustic potash are the best known of the chemicals called alkalis. They form a solution in water that is very bitter to the taste and feels slippery or soapy. And they are in fact used to make soaps—soda for hard soap, potash for soft soaps. Caustic soda is used in making paper and rayon, too.

The proper names for these alkalis are sodium hydroxide and potassium hydroxide. They are called *caustic* because they can burn and destroy body tissue.

Chemically, alkalis are strong bases—substances which combine with, or *neutralize,* acids to form salts (see Acids). One of the weaker alkalis is ammonium hydroxide, or common household ammonia.

Alloys Few pure metals have all the properties we require of a metal. But we can usually improve the properties of a pure metal by adding other metals to it to form a mixture called an *alloy*. For example, copper is soft and fairly weak but we can add zinc to it to form brass, or tin to form bronze, both of which are hard and strong. Aluminium, too, can be greatly strengthened by adding copper to it. In fact, most alloys are stronger than the parent metals.

Steel, the best-known alloy, consists of a mixture of a metal—iron—not with another metal but with the non-metal carbon. Other metals are added to steel to produce the most important of all alloys—the alloy steels.

Metals for alloying are chosen and mixed so that the alloy has the combined best properties of both metals. Stainless steel, for example, has the strength of steel and is stainless like the chromium it contains. By themselves, steel will rust and chromium is not strong.

The properties of alloys can usually be further improved by methods of heat treatment, such as annealing (heating and cooling slowly) and quenching (heating and dipping in cold water or oil).

Alphabet This is a group of characters or symbols used to write down a language. English is written in the *Roman* alphabet with 26 letters. Most other European languages are written in this alphabet, but the actual characters or letters may be pronounced in different ways. The 26-letter alphabet is not large enough for some of these languages, and accent marks are added to the letters to show differences in pronunciation. In French, accented letters include *é, è, à* and *ç*; and in

An alloy is a mixture of two or more metals. The metals are chosen and mixed in such a way that the alloy combines their best qualities.

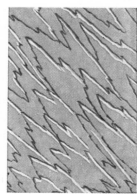

Metals mix in different ways. They may remain quite separate in the alloy, with crystals of one embedded in crystals of the other (top left). They may mix slightly, so that the crystals of one metal contain traces of the other metal (top right). Or they may dissolve in each other completely (bottom right).

wun dæ a dog felt very pleeꝶd wiþ himself becauꝶ hee had a luvly, big, juesy peeꝶ ov meet, and hee desieded tω tæk it tω a plæs whær hee cωd enjoi it. on þe wæ hee crosst a streem bie a narrœ bridʒ and pauꝶd tω lωk in þe wauter. tω his disgust hee sau þær a dog liek himself wiþ an eeven bigger and nieser peeꝶ ov meet. sœ hee droppt his œn meet and pounst on þe uþer dog'ꝶ meet, and found himself floundering in þe streem wiþ nœ meet at aull.

Above: An example of the Initial Teaching Alphabet which has been designed to teach children to read.
Right: A comparison of the characters in the Arabic, Hebrew, Greek, Cyrillic and Latin alphabets.

German ä and ö. Additional letters may be used, such as the German ß (which stands for *ss*) and the Danish ø. Some languages use a Roman alphabet of less than 26 letters. Serbo-Croat dispenses with *q, w, x* and *y*; the Hawaiian language uses only 12 letters.

There are several other alphabets in common use. The *Greek* alphabet has 24 letters. It is used only in Greece, although scientists use the letters as symbols in their work. The word 'alphabet' comes from its first two letters: A *(alpha)* and B *(beta)*. Russians and other Slavs use the *Cyrillic* alphabet, which was developed from Greek about 1,100 years ago. Gaelic is written with an alphabet of 18 letters derived from the Roman alphabet. All these alphabets contain symbols for vowels and consonants. But the Arabic and Hebrew alphabets have symbols for consonants only. Vowels are indicated only by accent marks, and often never used at all.

Some languages can be written in two alphabets. Serbo-Croat is written in the Roman alphabet in one part of Yugoslavia and in the Cyrillic alphabet in another. And alphabets have been changed. In 1928, the Turks changed from using the Arabic alphabet to a Roman alphabet. New phonetic alphabets have now been designed to help children learn to read.

Arabic	Hebrew	Greek	Cyrillic (Russian)	Latin
ا	א	α	а	A
ـب	ב	β	б	B
س, ث	כ, ס	κ, σ	к, с	C
د	ד	δ	д	D
ع	ע	ε, η	е, э	E
ف	פ	φ	ф, ө	F
ك	ג	γ	г	G
ه	ה	ʿ	г	H
ى	י	ι	и, й	I
ج	—	—	дж	J
ك	כ	κ	к	K
ل	ל	λ	л	L
م	מ	μ	м	M
ن	נ	ν	н	N
و	ו	ο, ω	о	O
ـ	פ	π	п	P
ق	ק	ϙ	—	Q
ر	ר	ρ	р	R
س	שׁ, ס	σ, ς	с	S
ت, ط	ת, ט	τ	т	T
و	ו	υ	ы, ю	U
و	ו	υ	в	V
و	ו	F	—	VV
—	—	ξ	кс	X
ى	י	ι, υ	я	Y
ظ, ز	ז, צ	ζ	з	Z

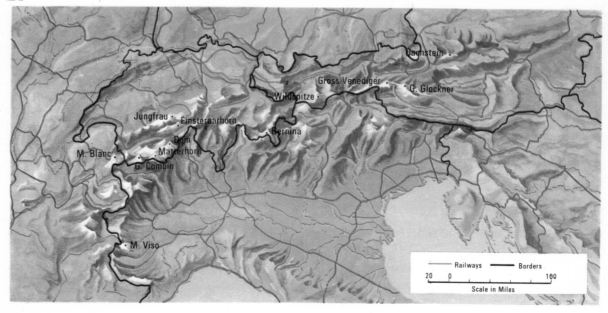

Alps The Alps are the greatest mountain system in Europe. They form an arc stretching for 680 miles from the Mediterranean in the west to the Adriatic in the east. They are between 80 and 140 miles wide and cover some 80,000 square miles. Their average height is 6,000 to 8,000 feet above sea level, but many peaks soar well above 10,000 feet.

Starting in France, by the Mediterranean, the Alps curve northwards, forming the border between France and Italy. They form the northern barrier to Italy and continue eastwards through Switzerland, southern Germany, and Austria. Finally, they turn southwards into Yugoslavia.

The main ranges are divided into Western, Central, and Eastern Alps. The *Western Alps* are those lying west of the Great St. Bernard Pass. The *Central Alps* are those between the Great St. Bernard Pass and Lake Constance. The *Eastern Alps* lie to the east of Lake Constance.

Alpine peaks, although not high by Asian and American standards, have presented formidable challenges to mountaineers. Mont Blanc (15,781 ft) is the highest mountain in Europe. Other well-known peaks are Monte Rosa (15,217 ft) and the Matterhorn (14,685 ft). The Eiger

The Alpine scenery, together with its opportunities for climbing and winter sports, attracts many tourists. The Alps have been called the 'playground of Europe'.

(13,042 ft) has an almost vertical rock wall for more than 7,000 feet.

Well-known Alpine tunnels and passes include the Little St. Bernard (a pass between France and Italy), the Great St. Bernard, St. Gotthard and Simplon (passes between Switzerland and Italy), and the Brenner Pass (between Austria and Italy). Two of the most recent road tunnels are the Mont Blanc, between France and Italy, and the Great St. Bernard tunnel, between Switzerland and Italy.

The Alps support a thriving tourist industry. Some of the best-known resorts where people go for winter and summer sports are Davos, Zermatt and St. Moritz in Switzerland; Innsbruck and St. Anton in Austria; Chamonix in France; and Cortina and Bolzano in Italy.

Aluminium In the early 1800's aluminium was virtually unknown and was regarded as a precious metal much dearer than gold. But it has now become one of our commonest and most useful metals.

Aluminium's most outstanding property is its lightness. It is only one-third as heavy as steel. And some of its alloys with copper and magnesium are as strong as steel. Aluminium and its alloys are therefore especially useful where lightness and strength are important, such as in aircraft, vehicles and ships. In addition, aluminium does not rust like steel, and it can be easily shaped.

Aluminium and its alloys are used for cooking vessels because they conduct heat well. They also conduct electricity well and are used for overhead power cables.

There is more aluminium in the Earth's crust than any other metal. But the only suitable ore is bauxite, which contains alumina—aluminium oxide. The metal is obtained by passing electricity through a solution of alumina in molten cryolite.

Amazon is the greatest river in South America. It is the second longest river in the world (only the Nile is longer), but it carries a greater volume of water than any other river. The Amazon is 3,900 miles long and, with its tributary the River Tocantíns, it drains an area of nearly 2¾ million square miles—almost half the South American continent. It provides about 30,000 miles of navigable waterways.

The Amazon rises in the Andes Mountains, in Peru. It is formed by the meeting of two other rivers, the Marañón and Ucayali, which rise a mere 100 miles from the Pacific Ocean. As it flows through the forests of northern Brazil, the Amazon is fed by more than 500 other rivers. It eventually empties into the Atlantic, on the Equator, on the northern side of the island of Marajó. Its mouth is 200 miles wide, and the water there is more than 200 feet deep. The volume of water is so great that fresh water is found on the surface 40 miles out to sea.

Ocean-going ships can sail up the river for 1,000 miles, as far as the town of Manaus, and smaller ships can proceed for a further 1,000 miles to Iquitos in Peru. But beyond there navigation becomes difficult because of rapids. The average speed of the Amazon is 1½ miles an hour, but during the rainy season the river overflows its banks and floods thousands of square miles of land.

Some historians believe that the Spanish explorer, Francisco de Orellana,

Location map of the Amazon, showing the vast area of South America drained by the main river and its tributaries.

discovered the Amazon in 1541, but others think that another Spaniard, Vicente Pinzón, saw it when he reached Brazil in 1500.

American Indians The name 'Indians' was given to the native peoples of America by the explorer Columbus. When he discovered the New World in 1492, Columbus mistakenly thought that he had reached the shores of India.

American Indians are related to the Mongoloid race. Their ancestors migrated into America from Asia by way of the Bering Straits about 60,000 years ago, and they gradually spread over the whole of North and South America. By far the greater number were living in Mexico and Peru when the continents were discovered by European explorers, and they numbered some 13 millions in all.

Today, the only untouched groups are in the remote Amazonian forests. Their patterns of life and languages varied enormously, and over one thousand different tongues and dialects still survive, though they are slowly dying out.

The most famous Indians are those of North America. These were the natives of the great American Plains, wanderers and hunters of the bison, or buffalo. They were divided into tribes and often

Left: A Brazilian Indian chief. The features bear witness to the fact that these people are related to the Mongoloid race.
Right: Some Indians living in the depths of the Amazonian rain-forests have been untouched by modern civilization. They still lead a Stone Age way of life.
Below: North American Indian children. Many leave the reservations when they grow up.

warred with each other. They lived in tents made of buffalo skins, known as wig-wams. They wore *moccasins* (shoes of soft leather) and decorated their clothes with beads. They often wore elaborate head-dresses made of feathers. Even when they wore head-bands decorated with only one or two feathers, these were signs of rank or prowess. Their religion, though simple, was a high code of honour and respect for bravery and ability.

Today they live mainly on *reservations* (large areas of land which are reserved exclusively for their use). They have their own tribal chiefs and councils and run their own affairs to a large extent. Many of the younger Indians have been educated. They attend universities, later entering trades and professions, to become part of the wide North American society which recognises many different races and cultures.

Ammonia is a very valuable gas which is vital to the manufacture of artificial fertilizers. Ammonia, an alkali, combines with sulphuric and nitric acids to form ammonium sulphate and nitrate. These two salts are good fertilizers because they are rich in the nitrogen which plants need for growth. Nitric acid is itself made from ammonia. Some refrigerators have ammonia as a refrigerant.

Ammonia is made by a process in which nitrogen extracted from the air combines with hydrogen. It is also a by-product from the manufacture of coal gas. It is lighter than air and has a stinging smell.

Amoeba is a very simple kind of animal. It consists of a single cell, and belongs to the lowest division of the animal kingdom, the *protozoans* (see Protozoans).

An amoeba moves by extending a *pseudopod*—a finger-like projection of a jelly-like substance called *protoplasm* —in the direction of travel. The rest of the amoeba flows into the pseudopod. To feed, the amoeba extends pseudopods

around a food particle and engulfs it.

An amoeba is about 1/100 of an inch across. It reproduces by dividing into two new amoebae. Amoebae live in fresh and salt water, in soil, and in men and animals. One amoeba causes a type of dysentery in man.

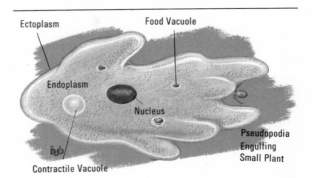

Ectoplasm | Food Vacuole | Endoplasm | Nucleus | Pseudopodia Engulfing Small Plant | Contractile Vacuole

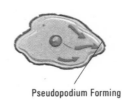

Pseudopodium Forming

Above: All the processes of life take place within the single cell of the amoeba. A large amoeba is just visible to the naked eye.

Left: An amoeba moves by the forward flow of its living material.

Below: An amoeba reproduces by dividing in two. First the nucleus divides, then the rest of the cell.

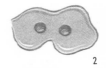

1   2   3   4

Amphibians are the class of animals that includes frogs, toads, newts, and salamanders. Amphibians first appeared on the Earth about 400 million years ago. They evolved from fishes that came out of the water and developed air-breathing lungs. Many amphibians are equally at home in fresh water and on land, but almost all amphibians breed in water. And if they

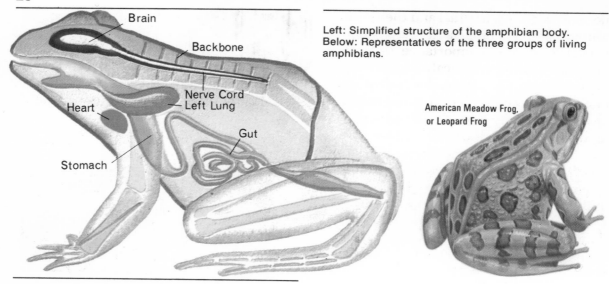

Left: Simplified structure of the amphibian body.
Below: Representatives of the three groups of living amphibians.

American Meadow Frog, or Leopard Frog

Marbled Salamander

South American Caecilian (Blindworm)

live on land, it is usually near water.

Most amphibians lay eggs that float in water or are attached to stones or water plants. The way in which the *larvae* (the young amphibians) grow into adults is like the evolution process by which amphibians came into being. A frog larva or *tadpole* has gills with which it obtains oxygen from the water to breathe. It swims by using its tail, like a fish. But as the tadpole grows, it loses its fish-like character. Lungs and limbs develop until it is able to leave the water and climb onto the land and breathe air.

Some amphibians, such as newts, spend most of their time in the water. Others, such as frogs and toads, are at home on land and in the water, and some, like the salamanders, live mainly on land.

Amphibians are cold-blooded animals and usually small in size, although the largest, the giant salamander of Japan, is six feet long. There are three main kinds of amphibians: tailed amphibians, tail-less amphibians, and caecilians.

Tailed amphibians include the newts and salamanders. Newts live mostly in water, whereas salamanders are found mainly on land. They have long tails and four short limbs, and are found all over the world except in polar regions.

Tail-less amphibians include frogs and toads. They have large and powerful hind limbs with which they propel themselves through water and to jump about on land. They, too, are found in most regions of the world.

Caecilians are legless amphibians. They live in burrows in moist soil. Some lay eggs, but others produce live young. Caecilians are found in tropical regions around the world.

Amsterdam is the capital, the largest city (pop. 867,000), and a port of the Netherlands (Holland). It lies close to the mouth of the River Amstel. Its large port is connected to sea by the 15-mile-long North Sea Canal. Another canal links it with the River Waal and the Rhine. With an extensive dock and quay system the port is of prime importance in European trade and communications.

The city is the acknowledged world centre of the diamond cutting and polishing industry and has important banking, insurance and ship-owning interests. It is also a thriving manufacturing city, active with shipbuilding, sugar refining, chemical manufactures and clothing. A feature of the city are its many canals and bridges. There are many fine buildings, among which is the Royal Palace, built in 1665. The Rijksmuseum contains the national collection of paintings. Rembrandt lived in the city and his house is now a museum. The Amsterdam Concertgebouw Orchestra has an international reputation.

Amundsen, Roald (1872-1928), was a Norwegian explorer. He was the first man to reach the South Pole. He also discovered the North-West Passage, a route round the north of Canada between the Atlantic and Pacific oceans that had been sought for hundreds of years.

Amundsen was an expert navigator and surveyor. In 1910, he set sail from Norway in the *Fram*, intending to drift with the ice floes towards the North Pole. He aimed to be the first man to reach it. But, just as he was about to start, he learned that the American Admiral Robert Peary had beaten him to it. So Amundsen turned his attention to the Antarctic and the South Pole.

In January 1911, he pitched camp on the ice at the Bay of Whales. In October, Amundsen and his party pushed inland with sleds and dogs. On the 14th December, 1911, they reached the South Pole, beating a British team under Captain Scott by four weeks.

In 1926, Amundsen flew across the North Pole in an airship piloted by Captain Umberto Nobile. Two years later, Nobile was lost on an Arctic expedition. Amundsen set out to look for him by air, and his plane disappeared without trace.

Above: Amsterdam is a bustling city famed for its canals, bridges and fine buildings.

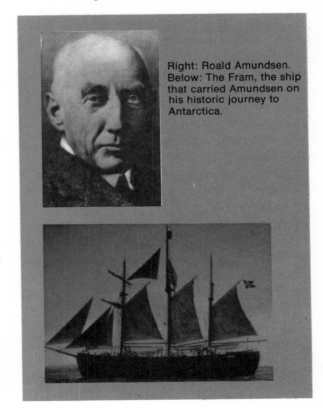

Right: Roald Amundsen. Below: The Fram, the ship that carried Amundsen on his historic journey to Antarctica.

Anaesthetics are substances used to prevent people from feeling pain when an operation is performed. Depending upon the type of operation, it may be necessary to put the patient into a deep sleep, or merely to deaden the pain on one small area of the body. An anaesthetic which causes unconsciousness is called a *general* anaesthetic, and one that affects only a specific area or locality is called a *local* anaesthetic.

Local anaesthetics are used a great deal in dentistry. If a badly decayed tooth is to be drilled, the dentist first injects the surrounding gum with a substance such as *Novocaine*. Within seconds, the area injected begins to grow numb.

In the cases where a general anaesthetic is used, the patient is usually put to sleep quickly by an injection into his veins of the drug *thiopentone*. During the operation, a gas, normally *halothane,* is inhaled by the patient. This ensures continued sleep.

Andes is the name of the great mountain system that runs down the western coast of South America. It stretches for more than 4,500 miles from Panama in the north to Cape Horn in the south, and is the world's longest mountain chain. Several peaks soar to more than 20,000 feet, and only the Himalayas in Asia are higher than the Andes.

Parts of the Andes run through Panama, Colombia, Venezuela, Ecuador, Peru, Bolivia, Chile and Argentina. For about half their length, the mountains are more than 12,000 feet high. From the point of view of the Earth's history, they are quite new mountains, but they have been severely affected by weathering. Fast-flowing rivers and enormous glaciers have produced many gorges and valleys. Most of the peaks are volcanic, and some are still active volcanoes.

The northern Andes split into three roughly parallel ranges. The central Andes extend up to 500 miles in width. They form plains that are 12,000 feet

high, and some of the highest peaks are found there. Among these are Chimborazo (20,577 ft), Cotopaxi (19,344 ft) and Ojos del Salado (22,590 ft). The southern Andes become lower as they approach Cape Horn, but they also contain Mt. Aconcagua (22,834), the highest mountain in the Americas.

The Andes are rich in minerals — copper, silver, and gold being the most important.

Angkor Wat The Angkor Wat is a superb temple of vast size and great architectural grandeur situated one mile to the south of the ancient walled city of Angkor Thom in what is now known as Cambodia. It is a masterpiece of the classical architecture of the Khmer Empire which flourished between A.D. 600 and 1434 in the region of Cambodia, Laos and Thailand. The temple was built around A.D. 1140 by King Suryavarman to celebrate many years of victorious

Left: The Andes run for 4,500 miles down the western edge of South America.

Below: The famous statue 'Christ of the Andes' stands high in the mountains on the Chile-Argentinian border. It was erected by the two countries to mark the peaceful settlement of a long-standing dispute and their intention never to wage war against each other.

fighting. It is adorned in low relief with
many scenes from the epics of the Hindu
religion. For many years the city and the
temple were lost in the forests but they
were re-discovered by French explorers
in 1861. The whole of this remarkable
Khmer Empire produced many fine
buildings and pieces of sculpture of which
the Angkor Wat is undoubtedly the most
famous.

Angling is fishing with rod and line, as
distinct from net fishing. The angler
employs his skill of casting with proper
equipment and lure to catch the fish.

It is estimated that about one person
in twenty-five in Britain and the U.S.A.
takes an active interest in coarse angling,
i.e. freshwater fish other than the salmon
family. Standard tackle for this is a cane
rod, about 12 feet long, a small reel
usually made of a light metal alloy, about
30 yards of silk line, a quill float, a level
gut cast about two yards long weighted

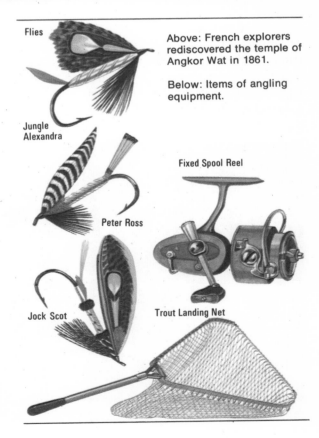

Flies

Jungle
Alexandra

Peter Ross

Jock Scot

Fixed Spool Reel

Trout Landing Net

Above: French explorers
rediscovered the temple of
Angkor Wat in 1861.

Below: Items of angling
equipment.

with split-shot, and a small hook with worm or maggot as lure.

To preserve supplies of fish in the rivers, various restrictions are imposed by local authorities and clubs. 'Close' seasons, when fish are spawning, must be respected.

The usual method of angling for trout and salmon, most prized of the fresh-water fish, is with artificial flies. Fly-casting is a highly specialised skill. A lighter, shorter and springier rod, often of split cane with a steel centre, is used.

Equipment for sea fishing must be stronger, and weighted more heavily because of the tide. Hooks are bigger, and sea creatures such as lugworms and shrimps are used for bait. The marine equivalent of salmon fishing is fishing for bass, the best fighter.

The Egyptians used line and bait to catch fish long before the Christian era, while the invention of the reel dates back to the 15th century. In 1653 Izaak Walton, 'patron saint of anglers', published his world-renowned book, *The Compleat Angler*.

Anglo Saxons In the fifth century A.D., Britain was attacked by fierce warriors from southern Denmark and northern Germany. They were called Angles and Saxons (after the Saex, or short sword, with which they fought). Britain was no longer defended by Roman soldiers and the Saxons found plenty of plunder. They conquered most of Britain except for the North and the West. The land they settled in came to be called England (Angle-land).

Above: A Saxon cross which has survived at Eyam, Derbyshire.

Left: A purse-lid from the Sutton Hoo treasure. The excavation of a burial ship at Sutton Hoo, Suffolk, in 1939, revealed the treasures of a Saxon king, including silver bowls and garnet-set gold jewellery. Forty gold coins date the burial to a period between A.D. 650 and 655.

The Saxons lived in tribes, each with its chief and warriors (thegns). Their laws were primitive, and each family avenged any wrong done to one of its members. They worshipped pagan gods such as Thor, the God of Thunder. The Saxons were skilled metalworkers, and beautiful examples of their craft were found at Sutton Hoo (Suffolk) in 1939. They lived in wooden buildings in small villages and avoided the stone villas and towns left by the Romans. The main building in each village was the chief's hall, which was often used for great feasts.

At first England was divided into Seven Kingdoms (the Heptarchy), but during the ninth century invasions (see Vikings) King Alfred united the Saxons. After this, the Kings of Wessex ruled over all England. In the seventh century, the Saxons had become Christians. Monasteries and churches were built. Saxon monks became skilled in the art of illuminating books. Learning spread, so that laws were written down. So were ancient poems, such as Beowulf, which had previously been sung by minstrels.

After 1066, England was not ruled by Saxon kings, but the language and customs of the Saxons continued to live on to shape the English way of life.

Animal Kingdom This is one of the two great sections into which biologists divide all living things. The other section is the plant kingdom (see Plants). In most cases, the differences between animals and plants are obvious. Animals, for instance, can move about under their own power, whereas plants cannot. Yet some microscopic plants can travel about in water by moving tiny hairs (see Algae). Again, animals eat plants or other animals, whereas plants make their own food or live on dead organic matter. Yet there are plants that catch and feed on insects (see Insect-eating plants).

There is a much greater variety of animals than there is of plants. Biologists know of nearly a million different species (kinds) of animals, but only about a third as many plants. Animals vary from the tiny one-celled amoeba—so small that it can be seen only under a microscope—to the huge blue whale, which may reach a length of 100 feet and a weight of 150 tons. Animals live in almost every part of the world: from the great depths of the oceans—where there are strange-shaped fish with glowing bodies—to high mountain regions. Animals even live in the bitter cold of the polar wastes and in the searing heat of the deserts.

One important difference between plants and animals is that most animals have far more accurate and sensitive senses (see Senses). They can learn more precisely what is happening in their surroundings, and react quickly to it. This is because they have some kind of nervous system. As a result, they can avoid danger and search for food and shelter. When the weather changes or a natural disaster such as fire or flood occurs they may be able to move to somewhere where the conditions are better. As a result, they have a better chance of survival. Animals can also *adapt* (change) to varying conditions more quickly. It is this great ability to adapt that has led to the great variety of animals. This has occurred through the process of evolution (see Evolution).

But, in spite of this variety, most animals have similar features to some other animals. Biologists use such similarities as the basis on which to classify animals into groups. The closer they are related—the more similar they are—the closer is the grouping. In this way, a number of species may be grouped into a single *genus*, several of which make up a *family*. Families are themselves grouped into *orders*. A number of orders make a *class*, and several classes comprise a *phylum*. The 20-odd phyla are the principal groups that make up the animal kingdom.

By far the biggest of these in terms of the number of species is the phylum *Arthropoda*, the arthropods. This includes all

Protochordata: Chordates that have no true brain and no braincase or backbone. They lack a heart and the type of kidney typical of vertebrates. Examples are the sea-squirts, lancelets and acorn worms.

Cyclostomata: Vertebrate chordates with an endoskeleton of cartilage. They have no jaws and lack scales and bones. Examples are the lampreys, hag fishes and slime hags.

Elasmobranchii: Fishes with well-developed jaws. They have an endoskeleton made of cartilage; bone is entirely lacking. The skin is covered with horny, teeth-like scales.

Choanichthyes: Fishes with internal nostrils. Their paired fins have fleshy lobes. Examples are the coelacanth and lung fishes.

Actinopterygii: Ray-finned fishes with well-developed jaws. They have an endoskeleton made almost entirely of bone.

Amphibia: Cold-blooded vertebrate animals that usually need to return to the water to breed. Except in some limbless forms, they lack scales. They usually have lungs and a moist skin through which they can breathe. Examples are frogs, toads, newts and salamanders.

Reptilia: Cold-blooded vertebrates fitted for life on land. The skin is dry and covered in scales. They have lungs and show an advance on amphibians in laying shelled eggs which hatch on land. Examples are crocodiles, snakes, turtles and lizards.

Aves: Warm-blooded vertebrates that have feathers. Like most reptiles they lay shelled eggs. Another reptilian characteristic is the presence of scales on the legs and feet. The fore-limbs are modified as wings.

Mammalia: Warm-blooded vertebrates that have hair. The young are nourished with milk which is provided by milk or mammary glands. Except for the monotremes which lay eggs, mammals bear their young alive.

Monotremata: The egg-laying mammals. Examples are the platypus and spiny ant-eater. Neither animal has teeth.

Marsupialia: The pouched mammals. These bear their young alive but in a small, relatively unformed state. The female has a pouch on the lower part of the abdomen in which the young are carried and suckled until they are able to fend for themselves. Examples are the kangaroos, wallabies, koalas and opossums.

Placentalia: Mammals in which the young during their early development are connected to the mother by a 'plate' of tissue—the placenta. This passes on food, oxygen and chemicals to the embryo. The young are born at a more advanced stage than in other mammals. Examples are the rodents, cats, dogs, horses, sheep, monkeys, apes and man.

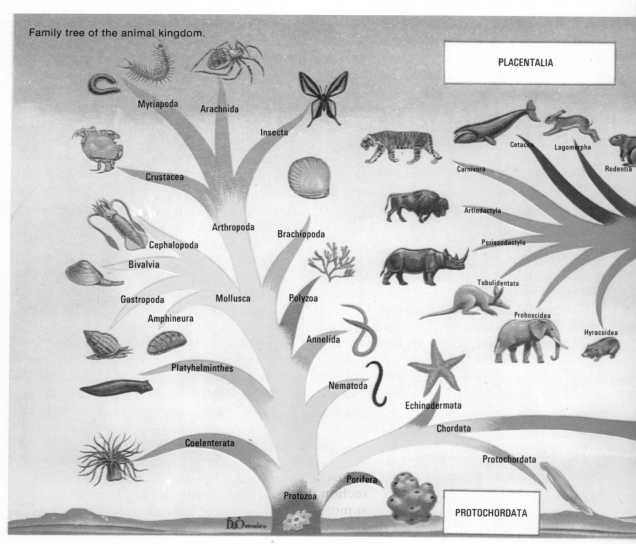

Family tree of the animal kingdom.

the insects, crustaceans, spiders, scorpions, centipedes and millipedes. These groups are themselves classes within the phylum. Insects alone number over 800,000 species—more than three-quarters of all the known species of animals.

Another important phylum is *Mollusca,* the molluscs. Most of these creatures have shells—examples include snails, clams, limpets, oysters and mussels. But some molluscs, such as the squid and octopus, have entirely soft bodies, with no shells.

Perhaps the most varied and most important phylum is the *Chordata,* the chordates. What distinguishes them from all other animals is the hollow nerve cord that extends the length of their backs. They also have some kind of supporting

rod of elastic material. In the more primitive chordates, this is a simple *notochord,* but the *vertebrates*—the most important group of chordates—all have backbones.

The vertebrates are the most advanced and most successful of all the animals. They include the fishes, amphibians, reptiles, birds and mammals. The mammals are the most advanced of the vertebrates, and the most advanced mammal is man himself: he is the most successful animal that has ever lived.

Annual plants are those that grow from seed, mature, flower, set their own seeds, and then die all within the space of one growing season. They are distinguished from *biennials,* which take two years to

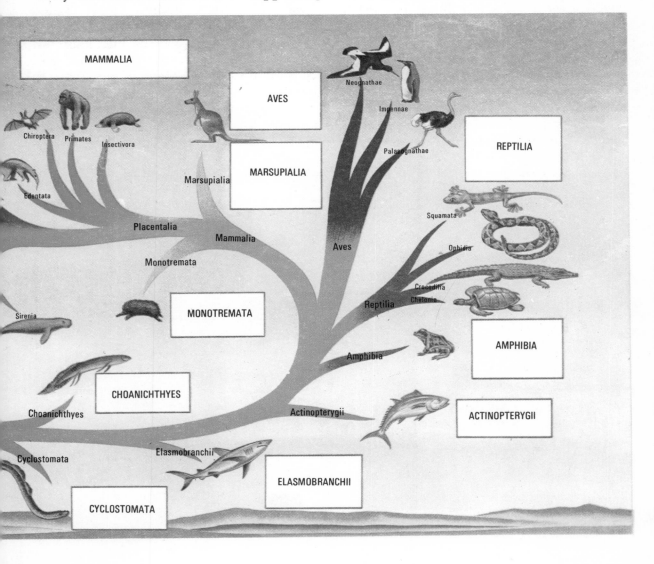

achieve a similar cycle, and from *perennials* which die back and grow again for a number of years. Familiar garden annuals include stocks, nasturtiums, petunias, godetias and asters.

Antarctica is the fifth largest continent in the world. It is a roughly circular land mass lying around the South Pole and surrounded by the Antarctic Ocean. With its area of about 5,100,000 square miles, Antarctica is larger than either Australia or Europe.

Until the 1900's, Antarctica was an empty wasteland, known to be the coldest place on Earth. The only people who live there today are whalers and scientists. This desolate region is almost completely covered by a great ice sheet. The ice is generally more than a mile thick and in places it is two-and-a-half miles thick. Most of the world's permanent ice is in this region. Blinding snow storms and fierce, icy winds make Antarctica a most unattractive place for all forms of life.

In a few places, mountain peaks called *nunataks* appear above the level of the ice. These peaks are part of great mountain chains that lie buried beneath the ice. Antarctica is very mountainous and some peaks rise to 16,000 feet.

The climate of Antarctica is extremely severe. The world's lowest temperature, $-126.9°$ F ($-88.3°$ C), was recorded there in 1960. In winter, temperatures often fall below $-70°$ F ($-57°$ C). Even in the summer, Antarctica is far colder than Arctic Ocean near the North Pole.

The only plant life found in Antarctica consists of some algae, lichens and mosses. But large numbers of penguins, petrels and seals live in some coastal areas. The ocean waters are rich in plant and fish life and whales are hunted in the seas that encircle the continent.

Antarctica was the last continent to be discovered and explored. The British seaman, Captain James Cook, sailed around the continent between 1772 and 1775. He did not reach the mainland, but saw much of the rich life in the seas. Hearing his reports, many sailors began to hunt seals and whales in the region.

In 1820 the coast of Antarctica was sighted. The first landing was probably made by an American sailor, John Davis, in 1821. The British explorer Robert Falcon Scott made the first major inland

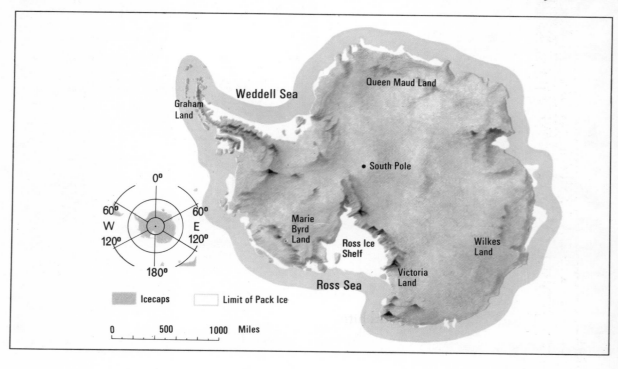

Above: Surveying in Antarctica. As yet large areas of this isolated continent remain unmapped.

Above right: Hidden crevasses are one of the greatest hazards to Antarctic travellers. Long, tracked pontoons help to spread a vehicle's weight over the ice, but accidents can still happen. This tractor was safely retrieved despite its perilous position.

Right: In temperatures around minus 50°F the emperor penguin rears its solitary chick. The egg, and later the chick, is supported on the adult penguin's webbed feet and protected from the cold by its thick feathers.

Below: An early-morning scene in Antarctica as a scientific expedition prepares to break camp. Mist hangs low over the desolate ice-shrouded landscape.

Left: Impala are always intensely alert and at the slightest sign of danger will flee in a magnificent series of leaps and bounds.

Right: The horns of the sable antelope sweep back from its black-and-white-striped face like a pair of scimitars.

journey in 1901–4. But the first man to reach the South Pole was the Norwegian Roald Amundsen, who planted his country's flag there on December 14, 1911. A British team led by Scott arrived about a month later. But Scott and his companions died in the cold on their return.

The development of aircraft speeded the exploration of Antarctica. In 1929 the American Richard E. Byrd became the first man to fly over the South Pole. In 1959 an agreement was signed by 12 nations ensuring the use of Antarctica for peaceful purposes only.

Ant-eaters are strange-shaped mammals living in South America. There are three main kinds: the giant ant-eater, which grows up to seven feet long; the lesser ant-eater, or tamandua, which reaches three and a half feet; and the pigmy ant-eater, about the size of a squirrel. All have extremely long snouts, tiny mouths,

The giant ant-eater stands about two feet high and may measure seven feet from snout to tail.

and long worm-like tongues. They eat mainly termites (white ants). They use the strong claws on their front feet to break open a termite nest, then lick up the insects with their tongues.

The spiny ant-eaters of Australia are primitive egg-laying mammals. They are quite unrelated to the South American ant-eaters.

Antelopes are herbivorous mammals, usually with long horns. They live mainly in Africa, but some species live in southern Asia. They generally live in herds on open grasslands or in areas with a few trees. They are very timid creatures, and run at the first sign of danger. They are extremely graceful when they run, often taking long, smooth leaps.

At first sight, antelopes may look rather like deer, but they are more closely related to goats, sheep and cattle than to deer. Deer, for instance, do not have true horns. Their branched antlers have a velvety covering and are shed each autumn and grow again each spring. Antelopes, on the other hand, have true horns that remain for life. They do not branch, and have a bony core with a covering of horn. (See Horns and antlers.)

There are many different species of antelopes. In some, only the male has horns, but both sexes usually have them. The horns are generally curved, and may curl in a spiral. Some kinds have ridged horns. Most antelopes have smooth, brown or grey hair. Many species have white or black markings, particularly white underparts. They all have hoofs.

The smallest antelope — the royal antelope — stands only 12 inches high at the shoulder. The gnu, on the other hand, reaches over four feet and weighs 500 lb. Some antelopes of South Africa can make huge leaps. The springbok, for example, can jump up 10 feet in the air when it is frightened. It then runs off at up to 60 miles an hour. The impala can cover 30 feet in a single leap, reaching a height of six feet.

Antibiotics are substances, produced by living things, which are poisonous to bacteria and other micro-organisms. A more general meaning for antibiotic is any substance which can restrict the growth of such micro-organisms. In medicine, antibiotics are used to destroy disease-producing bacteria, and also to prevent these bacteria from taking hold in a patient, and causing an infection.

For a long time, it was thought that any medicine that had the power to kill a particular microbe would also kill the patient under treatment. The first person to discover a drug that was both destructive and yet safe to administer was a scientist named Paul Ehrlich when he successfully used the compound salvarsan in 1909.

The next advance in antibiotics was the development of a group of drugs called the *sulphonamides*. These were a variety of compounds *synthesized* (made up) by chemists. The first one was put on the market in Germany, in 1935. It was a red dye, *Prontosil*, which had been proved experimentally to cure infections caused by a virulent streptococcus bacteria. Gerhard Domagk, the discoverer of Prontosil, soon learnt, however, that the dye itself was not necessary for treatment. The important ingredient was a simpler substance, one of the sulphonamides, contained in it. Used in the treatment of puerperal fever, a disease of women in childbirth, Prontosil reduced the death rate from 71% to zero.

A still more important discovery was to come. This was penicillin, not a synthetic substance, but one naturally produced by living moulds. Alexander Fleming, a British scientist, noticed in 1928 that some moulds that were growing amidst bacteria cultures were surrounded by a clear area. He confirmed by experiment that the juice from these penicillium moulds destroyed bacteria, but was absolutely harmless to animals. It was many years before penicillin was available for the treatment of diseases. The freshly extracted juice remained effective for only a few days, and experiments, by Fleming and other scientists, continued through World War II, before the drug became usable.

Penicillin is used in the treatment of pneumonia, and a great many other infections. Streptomycin, a more recent antibiotic, is used against tuberculosis.

Ants are found all over the world, except in polar regions, and there are about 3,500 different kinds. Ants are social insects — that is, they live and work in colonies, as do many bees and wasps. A colony of ants may consist of thousands of ants, each of which has its own particular duty to keep the colony going. Most ant colonies live in nests, either on the ground or in trees. Ant hills on the ground contain many chambers and tunnels con-

Ants communicate with one another by rubbing their feelers together.

necting them in which the ants store food and look after their young. A colony consists of a *queen* ant, *male* ants and *worker* ants.

The queen ant does nothing but lay eggs once she has started the nest, while the male ants' only duty is to mate with the queen. The actual running of the colony is carried out by the workers, small female ants that do not mate or lay eggs.

Above: The male, queen, soldier and worker of the harvesting ant.

Left: Some ants 'milk' greenfly by stroking them and obtain a sweet secretion called 'honeydew'.

Below: A group of leaf-cutting ants known as the Attini cultivate their own food. They grow fungus on beds of leaf particles stored in the nest.

The workers repair damage, build new parts onto the nest, collect the food and look after the eggs and young. Some ant species have special worker ants called *soldiers*. These use their powerful jaws to defend the nest from attack, either by other ants attempting to occupy the nest, or by birds in search of a feast. They can also sting an enemy by squirting an acid.

A colony is started by a queen after mating during a 'marriage flight' of male and female ants. The males soon die and the female loses her wings, as she finds a place to build a nest and lays eggs. These hatch to form a small colony of which the female becomes the queen. As workers build up the nest the colony grows in size and numbers. It may last for many years, with a new queen replacing the old one when she dies.

Ants' eggs are very small and hatch out into larvae. These are small maggot-like creatures, quite unlike ants in appearance. A larva grows and sheds its skin several times. After a few weeks, it becomes a pupa, sometimes forming a cocoon around itself. The pupa remains in this stage without eating and hardly moving, while its adult body forms. It then breaks out to emerge as an adult ant.

Apes are the most man-like of all animals. In fact, man is classed biologically with the apes in the *anthropoid* group. Unlike monkeys, apes have no tails. They are generally larger than monkeys. In general form, apes' bodies are much like man's, but their arms are longer and the legs shorter in proportion than a man's. Except for their faces, hands and feet, apes are covered in hair.

What most distinguishes the apes from other animals is their brain. They are the most intelligent creatures in the world apart from man. In captivity, they may acquire many almost-human habits. They can solve quite difficult 'problems' and can use sticks as primitive tools — to pull something within reach, for instance. In

Left: Gibbons' arms are so long that when standing upright they can touch the ground with their fingers.

Below: The body of the chimpanzee is more similar to that of man than any other animal.

Left: The gorilla is the largest of the apes, standing six feet high and weighing as much as 600 lb.

all apes, the co-ordination of hand and eye is well developed. They can use both hands and feet as we use our hands, to hold objects and do things.

There are four main types of apes, divided into two groups. The *lesser apes* comprise several species of gibbons. The more advanced *great apes* include the orang-utan, chimpanzee and gorilla. Chimpanzees and gorillas live only in Africa; the other species live in Asia. They all live in groups in forests, and eat fruit and other plant food.

Gorillas are by far the largest of the apes. They stand as high as a man and may weigh up to 600 lb—over 40 stone. They are immensely strong. Both they and chimpanzees live and move about on the ground, climbing to platforms built in trees to sleep. Chimpanzees can also swing from tree to tree, however. They are extremely intelligent animals, and have great curiosity. They love exploring.

Orang-utans are the only apes to live entirely in trees; they swing from branch to branch in the forests of Sumatra and Borneo, in Indonesia. Their name means 'man of the woods' and they may look re-markably human. Gibbons can also travel at great speed through the forests. They have extremely long arms and are smaller and lighter than the other apes.

Appalachians The Appalachians are a mountain system in eastern North America. They stretch 1,500 miles from Quebec Province (Canada) to Alabama (United States). The Appalachians contain some of the largest coalfields in the United States, and are heavily forested.

They may be divided into five main parallel regions. In the west are the *Allegheny* and *Cumberland plateaus*. They include the Catskills at their northern end. Then comes the *Ridge and Valley* section. Next to this zone is the great *Appalachian valley. The Blue Ridge* forms the eastern heights. There the highest peaks are found. They include Mt Mitchell (6,684 ft) in North Carolina, and the Black Brothers (6,690 ft and 6,620 ft). The fifth zone is the *Piedmont Plateau*. The rocks composing the Appalachians are millions of years old, and have been worn down by rivers and, in the north, by glaciers as well.

The Appalachians form a divide, separating the rivers that flow into the Gulf of Mexico from those that flow into the Atlantic Ocean. On the coastal plains to the east of the mountains stand the great cities of New York, Washington, Baltimore and Philadelphia.

In parts of the Appalachians gaps have been cut by rivers flowing into the Atlantic. The most important is the Hudson-Mohawk gap which leads from New York into the heart of the continent.

Apples are a common fruit. They grow in temperate regions around the world, but not in the tropics nor in polar regions. The world's leading apple-growing countries are the United States, Italy, Germany, Japan and France.

Like most common fruits, apples belong to the rose family of plants. Other members of this family include the pear, peach, plum, cherry, apricot, blackberry, strawberry and raspberry. Wild apples, called crab apples, are hard and sour. But over several centuries man has cultivated apples that are sweet to taste. Apple growers have produced many different kinds of apples of varying sweetness. They may also range in colour from light yellow through green to deep red, and in texture from hard and crisp to soft and juicy.

Apples are a good fruit to eat raw. They are about five-sixths water, the remaining sixth consisting of sugar, ascorbic acid (vitamin C) and other acids, and rough indigestible matter that gives the fruit its bulk. Apples are also used for cooking sweet dishes, and cider is brewed from fermented apples.

The apple is a common symbol in religion and legend. The forbidden fruit that Eve offered Adam in the Garden of Eden is usually thought to have been an apple.

Gathering the harvest in a New Zealand orchard. Apples grow in temperate regions around the world.

Exotic tropical fishes are fascinating to watch and easy to keep in a heated aquarium.

Aquarium is a tank for keeping fishes and other water animals. It usually has glass sides for viewing the inhabitants. A home aquarium can easily be made with a glass tank bought from a pet shop. The bottom should be covered with a layer of sand and gravel one or two inches deep, and clean water gently poured in. Place water plants in the tank—these will provide the fishes with oxygen. Plants include *Elodea, Vallisneria,* and *Sagittaria,* but many others can be used. The aquarium should be kept in a bright place, though not in sunlight, or provided with a light bulb. For tropical fish, the water should be kept at 70°F (21°C) with an electric heater.

An aquarium can support only a certain number of fishes. For every inch of a fish's body, there should be 20 square inches of water surface for tropical fish and 24 square inches for non-tropical fish. If there are too many fishes, there will not be enough oxygen in the water and some fishes will rise to the surface and gasp. These fishes should be removed or an aerator used to bubble air through the water.

Aquarium fishes can be fed with prepared foods from pet shops. Goldfish will eat insects. Fishes should be given no more than they will eat in 10 minutes, and uneaten food should be removed.

Marine fishes are more difficult to keep in an aquarium, but they will survive if continually provided with clean sea water. An aerator is necessary, and the aquarium should be kept in a cool and dim place. Marine animals picked up on the sea-shore, such as anemones and mussels, can also be kept in a marine aquarium.

Aqueduct Water often has to be transported from its source, such as a lake or river, to where it is needed for drinking, or irrigation, or for other purposes. The artificial channels built to carry the water are called *aqueducts*. The most familiar kind of aqueduct is an open channel carried by a bridge across a valley. But pipelines and tunnels are also classed as aqueducts.

The Ancient Romans were great builders of aqueducts, and many are still standing. One at Nîmes in France stands more than 150 feet high and has three tiers of massive stone arches.

A massive three-tiered aqueduct built by the Romans near Izmir, Turkey.

44

Arabia is a large desert peninsula of south-western Asia, which is almost completely separated from Africa by the Red Sea. Arabia is the earliest known home of the Arab people. From its two 'forbidden' cities of Mecca and Medina (forbidden to non-Muslims) sprang the religion of Islam.

Most of the peninsula forms the kingdom of Saudi Arabia. The sheikhdom of Kuwait lies at the north-eastern corner of Arabia, at the head of the Persian Gulf. Seven sheikhdoms — called Trucial Oman — the sultanate of Oman, and the sheikhdoms of Bahrain and Qatar occupy the eastern coast of Arabia. The republics of Yemen and Southern Yemen lie at the southern tip of Arabia.

Most of Arabia is a dry wasteland where rain seldom falls and few animals or plants live. Temperatures often top 130° F (55° C) during the daytime in summer, but the nights are cool.

Arabia's only railway connects Riyadh, Saudi Arabia's capital, with the Persian Gulf. Jedda, on the Red Sea, is an important sea and air port, handling pilgrims to Mecca and Medina.

Arabia came under Turkish rule in the 1500's. The British built a port at Aden in 1839, and by 1920 much of Arabia was under British influence. Until a generation ago, Arabia was one of the poorest and most remote places in the world. But geologists discovered petroleum in Arabia in the 1930's, and by the 1960's sales of petroleum had made Arabia rich. Saudi Arabia and Bahrain quickly developed socially and economically.

The transformation of Kuwait made possible by proceeds from petroleum was almost miraculous. The poor, sparsely-populated sheikhdom became, in the 1960's, one of the world's largest suppliers of petroleum and natural gas. It now possesses more wealth per head of its population than any other country.

Southern Yemen became an independent republic in November, 1967, following the union of Aden with other territories.

Arabs The Arab peoples came originally from the Arabian Peninsula, spreading until they founded a huge empire and culture, reaching from India to the shores

Above: An offshore drilling rig in the Arabian Gulf. Petroleum has brought great prosperity to Arabia.

Right: Location map of Arabia (marked in black).

Below: Modern Kuwait. Oil revenues have created sumptuous buildings and amenities in what was once an empty corner of the desert.

of the Atlantic Ocean. Today the name Arab is given to all the inhabitants of the peninsula, and also to all people who speak Arabic, and claim their descent from the original Arab conquerors. They live chiefly in northern Africa and Iraq (formerly called Mesopotamia).

The great majority of these peoples are followers of the Muslim religion, and it was the zeal and inspiration of this belief which drove the Arabs to extend their empire from A.D. 650 to 850.

Today, Arabs are either town dwellers, peasants, or Bedouin. In towns, the Arabs are traders, craftsmen, shopkeepers, clerks and officials. The peasants live in villages and work small farms. Their life is hard, and their standard of living meagre. There are few modern methods or machines in use. In most places oxen still pull the ploughs, and camels and donkeys are the chief means of transport. The Bedouin are *nomadic* (wandering) tribes who breed and train camels. They

Arabs today are deeply conscious of their unity of language and religion. Gamal Abdul Nasser, the Egyptian head of state, is a leading figure in the upsurge of Arab nationalism.

live in tents which they set up for perhaps a month at a time as they move in search of water and grazing land. (See Bedouin.)

Arabs today are very conscious of their unity of language and religion, and are struggling to unify themselves politically, but deep differences still divide them.

Archaeology The archaeologist reconstructs the lives and activities of past peoples — how they made a living, what tools they used, what skills they had acquired, even what diseases afflicted them. The clues for building up these pictures are the traces such peoples have left behind — bones, tools, ornaments, pottery and buildings.

The fractured bones of fallen warriors may reveal just what types of weapons were used in past warfare. Diseases may also leave their mark on the skeleton. The teeth of past peoples may reveal something of their diet. People who eat mainly meat rarely have rotten teeth. As the quantity of grain in the diet rises there is a tendency for tooth-decay.

Bones of animals may often be found associated with human communities, and their identification usually goes a long way to establishing the staple human diet. The remains may be of animals known to move from pasture to pasture — reindeer and bison, for instance. Almost certainly the human community also led a wandering existence.

The archaeologist works mainly by excavating a deserted site, from which he collects all the evidence of human occupation. Excavation today is a highly professional and scientific business, though the voluntary help of amateurs is often welcome. Often it is not possible to dig up the whole site, so the excavator plans trenches across it, perhaps at the corners, or straight through the middle. Each trench is marked out and its position on the map recorded. The trench is then sunk until virgin soil, earth untouched by man, is reached. First, the top layer of soil is carefully removed. Then each level or layer of earth underneath is carefully scraped away with builders' trowels. Different layers are revealed by changes in the colour of the soil. The position of everything found is carefully recorded, and important finds are photographed in position.

From these records the archaeologist draws plans of what was found in each level. Objects from the lower levels will be older than objects from the higher ones.

46

The archaeologist knows that one kind of broken pottery is older than another kind. But how much older? Occasionally a coin with a date is found with a particular type of pottery in one place. This gives a date for that kind of pottery wherever it is found. But much archaeology depends on arranging artefacts (pottery, flints, brooches, jewellery) into types, and trying to decide which type developed out of which other type, and when.

Recently a whole series of scientific techniques have aided the archaeologist to date his finds. One of the most accurate is the carbon-14 method. Carbon-14 is a radioactive form of carbon found in plants and animals. When living things die the radioactive carbon that has been taken in *decays,* breaking down to form nitrogen. The rate of this breakdown is constant. After 5,568 years half of the radioactive carbon has decayed. After another 5,568 years half as much again has disappeared. By measuring the quantity of radioactive carbon left in old wood, bones, peat, antlers and grain their age can be estimated.

A method of telling the relative age of human and animal remains involves testing the amount of fluorine they contain. Bones and teeth buried in the ground gradually absorb traces of fluorine. If bones found together contain the same amount of fluorine they are of the same age. This method proved the Piltdown skull to be a fake. Some of the bones were much younger than others.

Not all archaeology is done by excavating. By looking at a photograph taken from an aircraft we may discover the shape of a vanished building. Over the foundations crops will grow differently from crops on undisturbed ground. This difference will show clearly from the air.

Archaeology has revealed the secrets of ancient societies. It is also telling us new things about more recent times. Industrial archaeology is the study of old factories, mines and machinery.

Above: Modern archaeology is an activity requiring team-work and patience. Much of the work is carried out by voluntary helpers.

Left: Roman bronze cavalry helmet from Ribchester, Lancs. (late first century A.D.).

Below: Golden necklet from Caernarvonshire, Wales (*c.* 1700-1500 B.C.).

Archery The art of shooting with bow and arrow, also known as *Toxophily*, dates back to the Stone Age. Originally used for hunting, and in war, it first developed as a sport about the fourth century A.D. and has since enjoyed interest in various countries—particularly in Britain and the U.S.A.

The most popular form of the sport is *target shooting*. The standard British target is circular, four feet in diameter. In the centre is a golden circle (the pinhole) counting 9 points, and this is ringed by four concentric bands of (counting outwards) red (7 points), blue (5 points), black (3 points) and white (1 point). Scoring on an International Target is from 10 points for an inner gold to 1 point for an outer white (the colours themselves are divided on this target).

Any type of hand-bow may be used, the simplest being the 6-foot English longbow of yew. The arrow is feather-flighted and about 28 inches long, depending on an archer's draw length.

The earliest modern contest was held in Yorkshire, England, in 1673. In the U.S.A. the United Bowmen of Philadelphia was formed in 1828, and the first tournament was held in Chicago in 1879.

Archimedes (287?-212 B.C.) was a Greek mathematician and inventor. He achieved advances in science unequalled for hundreds of years. Among his discoveries was the principle of buoyancy— an object placed in a liquid experiences an upthrust equal to the weight of liquid displaced. Legend has it that Archimedes discovered this when he stepped into a full bath and saw water spilling over the sides. He rushed out into the

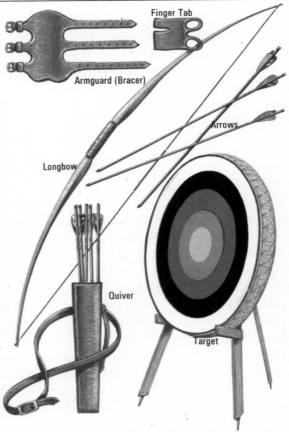

Left: The correct stance for target shooting, the most popular form of archery.

street crying 'Eureka' (I have found it).

He also worked out the laws of levers and pulleys. These showed that heavy loads could be moved with a small force. Archimedes regarded his calculations of the areas of circles and other curves as his most important work. Much of it is still basic to mathematics today.

Archimedes was born and lived in Syracuse, Sicily. During the long Roman seige of the city, the enemy was held back by catapults which Archimedes invented. When the Romans finally entered the city, their general ordered his men to spare Archimedes. But he was killed by a soldier who failed to recognize him.

Architecture is the art and science of designing buildings. Man's basic needs have always been threefold: food, clothing and shelter. Before recorded history man was a hunter, moving from place to place in search of food, and living in natural caves or under the rough shade of trees. The story of architecture began when he started to grow crops and tend cattle. Only then did man look for ways to build shelters that would keep him safe from bad weather, wild beasts, and human enemies.

Architecture reflects the progress of mankind. It is the story, in brick and stone, wood and metal, of people and their ways of life. Architecture as we know it today began in the Nile valley of Egypt about 6,000 years ago, and we can still see its influence in some of our present-day buildings.

Egyptian architecture began about 5,000 B.C. and ended in the first century A.D. The Egyptians, who left several massive pieces of architecture for us to examine, were often more interested in building tombs and temples than dwelling houses. The Sphinx, the Pyramids and other large monuments were enormously strong and built to last for thousands of years. The most famous Egyptian temple, at Karnak, was built in about 1200 B.C. and was made of stone. Most of Egypt's

---

Important Dates in the Development of Architecture

B.C.
3200 Rise of Ancient Egyptian Kingdoms. EGYPTIAN PERIOD begins. Great Pyramid of Cheops; Great Sphinx.
3000 Early Greek civilization
1800 Stonehenge begun
 700 GREEK DORIC
 525 Egypt becomes a Persian province
 400 GREEK IONIC and CORINTHIAN
 147 ROMAN PERIOD begins
 146 Romans conquer Greece
  30 Egypt conquered by Rome

A.D.
 300 BYZANTINE PERIOD begins (Eastern Roman Empire)
 400 EARLY CHRISTIAN PERIOD begins
 500 Roman Empire begins to collapse
 800 Crowning of Charlemagne ROMANESQUE PERIOD begins (in Northern Europe)
1066 NORMAN PERIOD begins (in England)
1140 GOTHIC PERIOD begins (in France, First Gothic building, Choir of St. Denis, near Paris)
1175 NORMAN PERIOD ends (in England), Canterbury Cathedral is rebuilt bringing Gothic architecture to England EARLY ENGLISH PERIOD begins
1200 ROMANESQUE PERIOD ends (in Northern Europe) HIGH GOTHIC PERIOD begins (in France)
1245 Building starts on Westminster Abbey
1250 LATE GOTHIC and FLAMBOYANT PERIOD begins (in France)
1299 DECORATED PERIOD begins (in England)
1330 Choir of Gloucester Cathedral built (first building in Perpendicular style) PERPENDICULAR PERIOD begins (in England)
1400 EARLY RENAISSANCE PERIOD begins (in Italy)
1485 TUDOR PERIOD begins
1500 HIGH RENAISSANCE PERIOD begins (in Italy Michelangelo)
1530 FRENCH RENAISSANCE PERIOD begins
1558 ELIZABETHAN PERIOD begins
1600 BAROQUE PERIOD begins (in Italy)
1603 JACOBEAN PERIOD begins
1650 BAROQUE PERIOD begins (in France)
1666 Fire of London Rebuilding of London by Christopher Wren BAROQUE PERIOD begins (in England)
1715 GEORGIAN PERIOD begins
1750 ROCOCO PERIOD begins (in France)
1811 REGENCY PERIOD begins
1837 VICTORIAN PERIOD begins
1920 MODERN ARCHITECTURE

N.B. Since the styles of architecture changed quite slowly, the dates given above are, in most cases, only approximate.

Right: Examples of stages in the development of architecture.

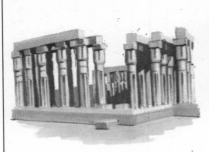

Egyptian: Temple of Amenhotep III (Luxor)

Greek Doric: Temple of Neptune, Paestum

Roman: Arch of Constantine, Rome

Byzantine: Santa Sophia, Constantinople

Romanesque: Pisa Cathedral

French Late Gothic: St. Ouen, Rouen

Italian Gothic: Milan Cathedral

English Decorated: York Minster

Roman Renaissance: St. Peter's, Rome

Baroque: Santiago de Compostela,

Anglo-Classic: St. Paul's Cathedral

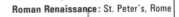

Modern: Empire State Building, New York

smaller buildings were made of baked clay and reeds.

Greek architecture began about 700 B.C. and lasted until the country was conquered by the Romans in the second century B.C. The Greeks tried to be perfect in everything they did. They constructed their buildings on a simple column-and-lintel method. Rows of columns held up flat beams (lintels), on which the roof was placed. They worked out the details and proportions of their architecture carefully and built so well and so perfectly that their buildings are considered the finest and most beautiful ever to be erected.

When the Romans conquered Greece they copied the Greek architectural styles. However, the Romans had discovered how to make an arch, and could make larger buildings. The Romans used the Greek Orders of Architecture. These were the Doric, Ionic and Corinthian Orders, and were the styles, or decorations, of the column-and-lintel way of building. The fall of the Roman Empire ended what is now called the Classical

The Sydney Opera House is an example of the revolution in architectural design made possible by modern construction materials.

period of architecture, a period which began with the rise of Greek architecture.

In A.D. 800 the Romanesque period of architecture began. This was a style that imitated ancient Rome, but slowly took on its own character. The Norman architecture of England was late Romanesque. In 1140 the great Gothic period began in France, and came to England in about 1175. In 1200 the High Gothic period, with its tall cathedral towers and soaring masonry, began in France and spread through Europe, at about the time of Early English architecture in Britain. The Decorated style in England began at the end of the 13th Century. Buildings became more elaborate, covered with stone ornaments, and had pointed windows.

In about 1400 the architects of Italy decided to build in the old Roman style again, and the Renaissance (the word means re-birth) began. Soon this new style from ancient days spread throughout

Europe. Later, many famous architects started to change it to fit in with the times, and Baroque architecture was born.

Victorian architecture was due to another revival of ancient days. This time it was the Gothic style. New materials, such as iron, were used to give Victorian buildings a character of their own, one that was often thought very ungainly and fussy.

Modern architecture began about 1920, and was the result both of new materials, such as re-inforced concrete and, later, plastics, and new ideas from bold and talented architects.

The colourful clothing of the Lapps who live in the far north of Scandinavia is a marked contrast to the bleak Arctic landscape.

Arctic The Arctic is the cold region around the North Pole. It includes the Arctic Ocean, which has an area of about 5,444,000 square miles. During the winter, pack-ice covers most of the Arctic Ocean. The ice is continually in motion, and as it grinds together large pressure ridges form. In the spring the ice begins to melt. Stretches of open water *(leads)* appear between the floes, and lakes form on the surface of the ice.

The Arctic also includes many islands, and parts of northern Asia, Europe and North America. This region is called the *tundra*. Trees cannot grow there because it is too cold. Snow covers the tundra during the winter. Temperatures then average $-30°$ F $(-34°$ C). During the short summer, temperatures rise to about $45°$ F $(7°$ C).

During the summer thaw, many plants and flowers grow. Plants include grasses,

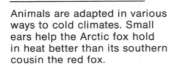

Animals are adapted in various ways to cold climates. Small ears help the Arctic fox hold in heat better than its southern cousin the red fox.

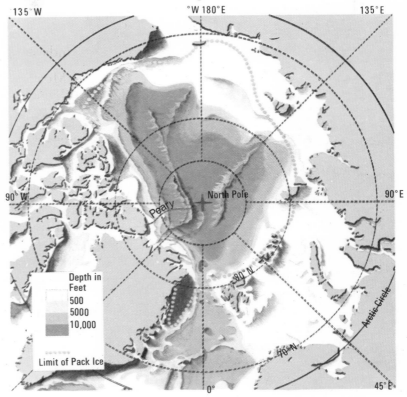

Depth in Feet
500
5000
10,000

Limit of Pack Ice

135°W
°W 180°E
135°E
90°W
90°E
North Pole
Peary
80°N
Arctic Circle
0°
45°E

mosses and low shrubs. Reindeer and caribou graze in the Arctic in summer, but travel south in winter. Other animals include bears, ermine and foxes.

The largest group of people living in the Arctic are the Eskimos, who hunt and fish. In winter, some live in snow houses called *igloos*. Others live in half-buried huts. (See Eskimos.)

Arctic exploration began with the Vikings and continued in the 16th century, when Europeans sought north-east and north-west routes to Asia. But by the time that the routes were discovered, about 300 years later, other far easier sea-routes to Asia were known.

In 1909, a team led by the American Robert E. Peary became the first men to reach the North Pole. The first man to fly over the Pole was another American, Richard E. Byrd, in 1926. Today aircraft regularly fly over the Arctic region. In recent years many scientists have worked in the Arctic. For example, in 1968, a British team set out to cross the Arctic Ocean on drifting ice. They studied the climate, wild life and many other things.

Argentina is South America's second largest country. With Chile, it forms the southern part of the continent. It is a long, wedge-shaped country, bounded on the east by the Atlantic Ocean. Its western frontier with Chile runs through the Andes Mountains.

There are five main regions of Argentina. The Gran Chaco, in the north, is a grassy plain, liable to floods near the rivers and to a shortage of water away from them. Few people live there. South and west of the Gran Chaco is an arid area of rough country and low rainfall, where a few hardy plants and cacti grow. But there are large fertile areas where people grow sugar, fruit and grapes.

East of the arid area lie the Pampas and Argentine Mesopotamia, huge fertile grassy plains covered by wheat and cattle farms. Patagonia, the southern part of Argentina, is largely desert. It has violent

Above: The grassy plains of eastern Argentina (the Pampas) support large herds of beef cattle. Meat is one of the country's chief exports.

Left: Location map of Argentina (marked in black).

Facts and Figures
Area: 1,072,000 square miles.
Population: 23,035,000.
Capital: Buenos Aires.

winds and little rain, and its winters are cold and unpleasant.

Most Argentinians are of Spanish and Italian descent, and speak Spanish. There are a few American Indians and *mestizos*, people of mixed Indian and European ancestry. Most people are Roman Catholics. The country is a republic, ruled by a president. Since 1966, he has made all laws himself.

Farming is the main source of Argentina's wealth. The country exports great quantities of beef, mutton, wheat and other cereals, and sugar. Argentina produces natural gas and petroleum.

Spanish settlers colonized Argentina, then called the Rio de la Plata, in the early 1500's. The country remained under Spanish rule until the early 1800's, when the colonists, led by José de San Martín, rebelled. Argentina became independent in 1816. It had a succession of elected governments until the 1960's, when the army nominated the president.

Bust of Aristotle, the Greek philosopher and scientist.

Aristotle was a Greek philosopher and scientist who lived four hundred years before the birth of Christ. His father was court physician to the king of Macedon. From his father, Aristotle received a good education in natural science.

When he was seventeen years old, Aristotle went to Athens, where he studied philosophy with Plato for twenty years. After Plato's death he returned to Macedon to become the tutor of Alexander the Great. Through Aristotle, Alexander learned to love and respect the Greek language and the Greek way of life.

When Alexander became king, in 336 B.C., Aristotle returned to Athens as a teacher. Unlike his own teacher, Plato, Aristotle did not believe that beyond the real world which man experiences with his senses there is an ideal world which man can experience only with his mind. He believed that man must learn from what he can see, hear, taste, touch, and smell. He taught his students to examine the world around them in detail. Aristotle's thinking was far more systematic than Plato's.

Aristotle's writings span every area of human learning known at the time he lived. His ideas have been an important influence in the development of philosophy, political thought, psychology, natural science, and the criticism of drama.

Armada This is the name given to the Spanish fleet which attempted an invasion of England in 1588 during the reign of Queen Elizabeth I. England and Spain were enemies for the latter part of the 16th century. English seamen such as Drake attacked Spanish treasure ships in South America. Finally, King Philip II of Spain decided to invade England. He collected a fleet at Cadiz. In 1587 this was attacked in harbour by Sir Francis Drake and the invasion had to be put off for a year.

An engraving representing the sharpest engagement that took place between the English and Spanish fleet against the Isle of Wight on July 25, 1588.

In 1588 a large fleet assembled at Lisbon. There were 130 ships and 30,000 men, of whom 19,000 were soldiers. The force was commanded by the Duke of Medina Sidonia. The plan was for the fleet to sail from Spain across the Bay of Biscay and up the English Channel. Off the coast of the Netherlands the fleet would embark Spanish soldiers from the army there. The force would then invade England and depose Queen Elizabeth.

The English prepared for action and the main fleet under Lord Howard of Effingham moved to Plymouth. The Armada left Lisbon at the end of May but ran into storms and had to return to Spanish ports, finally leaving northern Spain in July 1588. When the Armada entered the Channel, the English fleet came out from Plymouth and attacked the Spanish ships. But the Spanish ships sailed close together, forming a large crescent, and the English attacks did not stop their advance.

On July 28, the Spanish fleet anchored off Calais but the English created great confusion by setting old ships on fire and sending them among the Spaniards. The Spanish fleet lost its formation and was defeated on the following day in a general battle with the English fleet. The wind blew strongly from the south-west and the Spanish ships were forced to sail northwards and then round the coasts of Scotland and Ireland to get back to Spain. Many ships were wrecked on the way. Finally, broken ships and weary sailors returned to Spanish ports — the wreck of the 'Enterprise of England'. Only half the ships that set out came back. The defeat struck a great blow at Spanish prestige.

Armadillos are strange mammals of Central and South America. Their backs are covered with armour, consisting of closely-fitting bony plates. In spite of this armour, armadillos are nimble creatures. Some species can roll themselves up into a ball when attacked, the armour giving them complete protection. Armadillos have strong claws, particularly the giant armadillo, which grows up to four feet long. They use their claws to dig a burrow in which to live, and to smash open termite nests and ant-hills. These insects — together with earthworms, spiders and snails — form the armadillo's main food.

Bony armour protects the armadillo from its enemies.

Armour is special clothing that protects the wearer against an enemy's weapons. The earliest armour was made of animal skins and leather. It gave the wearer some protection against arrows, spears and clubs. Then men made metal shields, helmets and breast-plates. The rest of the body was still protected by leather or by a kind of fine wire-mesh called chain mail. During the Middle Ages, when knights rode into battle, armour became more elaborate. It covered the arms, legs, hands and feet. There was even armour for horses, and in India men rode on armoured elephants. Arrows and swords could not pierce the metal armour, and so some knights fought with great iron clubs and maces. Armourers covered armour with decorations. Painting, engraving, and even gold and gems glistened on the armour, although the most ornate suits were worn only for show.

As soon as soldiers became armed with muskets and pistols, armour was abandoned because bullet-proof armour could not be made light enough to wear. For hundreds of years, only the helmet continued in use as armour. Then during and after World War II, new materials were developed. Tough metals and plastics were used to make armour. Airmen on bombers wore flak-suits to protect them against flying splinters of metal. Soldiers wore

Roman Legionary
1st Century A.D.

English Knight
Early 14th Century

Austrian Knight
Late 15th Century

Italian Knight
Mid 16th Century

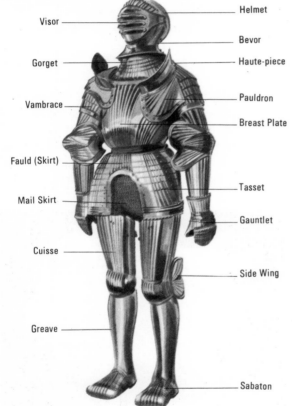

Visor — Helmet

— Bevor

Gorget — Haute-piece

Vambrace — Pauldron

— Breast Plate

Fauld (Skirt) —

Mail Skirt — Tasset

— Gauntlet

Cuisse —

— Side Wing

Greave —

— Sabaton

bullet-proof waistcoats made of over-lapping plastic or metal plates mounted on cloth like the tiles on a roof. Today some state leaders or policemen wear body armour to protect them against assassins' bullets. In modern warfare, *armour* is the name given also to an army's tanks and mobile guns.

In the Middle Ages, a full suit of battle armour weighed up to 70 pounds. It con-sisted of various pieces, some of which had curious names. A helmet completely covered the head, with a hinged *visor* at the front. The visor was normally open and lowered only in battle to protect the wearer's eyes. A collar protected the neck and joined the helmet to the shoulder piece. A breastplate and backplate cover-ed the body, with a *skirt* and *tasset* down onto the legs. Upper and lower leg-armour was called *cuishe* and *greave*. A mounted knight wore pointed steel shoes called *sollerets* and metal gloves called *gaunt-lets*. Foot soldiers also carried metal shields.

Some of the most ornate armour was made in Japan and other eastern countries. Japanese warriors called *samurai* wore armour for ceremonial occasions until a hundred years ago.

Arthropods belong to the *phylum* (major group) of animals called the *Arthropoda*. The name 'arthropod' comes from Greek words meaning 'jointed foot', but the legs are jointed as well as the feet. They also have bodies made up of jointed sec-

The ladybird and the centipede are both arthropods. They have jointed bodies and a hard outer covering.

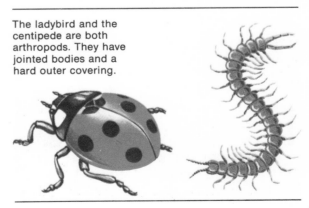

tions, with a hard outer covering called an *exoskeleton*. There is no internal skeleton. Arthropods make up about three-quarters of the world's animals. They include insects, crustaceans, spiders, and centipedes and millipedes.

Asbestos The special white suits that some firemen wear when fighting a fierce fire, such as an oil fire, do not catch fire because they are made of rock. A certain group of minerals are found naturally in the form of tiny fibres. They are all given the name of *asbestos*.

The longest of these fibres can be spun and woven into a fireproof cloth. Short-fibred asbestos is made into automobile brake and clutch linings, which have to withstand heat. Mixed with cement, it makes an excellent roofing material. With a suitable binder, it is used to insulate boilers and furnaces. Asbestos is a good electrical insulator, too, and is resistant to acids and alkalis.

By far the most important variety of asbestos is *crysotile*, or *white asbestos*. Asbestos rock may be mined on the surface or underground. The rock is sorted roughly by hand before passing through various crushing and screening (filtering) units, where first the long then the short fibres are extracted.

Top right: Raw amosite asbestos from South Africa.

Bottom right: Clutch plates. Asbestos, with its heat-resisting properties, is an important part of clutch facings and brake linings.

Below: An asbestos mine in Canada.

Asia is the largest of the continents and has more people than any other continent. It covers about 17,153,000 square miles—almost one-third of the land area of the world. Its greatest distance, east to west, is 6,000 miles, and north to south about 5,400 miles. Its population is about 1,887,500,000. This means that 57 out of every 100 people live in Asia.

Asia is a continent of extremes. It has the highest mountains and the lowest depths. Parts of the continent are colder than the North Pole but other areas are among the hottest places on Earth. More rain falls in parts of southern Asia than anywhere else in the world, but some Asian deserts are among the driest places on Earth.

Asia extends from the Ural Mountains in the west to the Pacific Ocean in the east: and from the Arctic Ocean in the north to the Indian Ocean in the south. Its south-western frontier with Europe runs along the shores of the Caspian Sea,

57

Black Sea and Mediterranean. Asia is
joined to Africa by the isthmus of Suez,
which is cut in two by the Suez Canal.
It is separated from North America by
the Bering Strait in the north-east, only
45 miles wide at its narrowest part.

Asia can be conveniently divided into
six major regions. *Central* or *Inner Asia*
is a triangular mass of mountains and high,
remote plateaus. It includes Tibet, Mongolia and parts of western China. Many
ranges of mountains meet in the *Pamir
Knot,* sometimes called the *Roof of the
World.* The Himalaya range includes Mt
Everest (29,028 ft), the world's highest
peak.

Northern Asia includes the vast Russian lowlands of Siberia. The region
stretches from the Ural Mountains in
the west to the Pacific Ocean in the east.
It is drained by a number of huge rivers.
Eastern Asia, or the *Far East,* is a mountainous area that includes most of China,
Japan, Korea, and Formosa. This is

Above: More than half of
the world's population
lives in Asia, but much
of the land is too moun-
tainous, too cold, or too
dry to grow crops. As a
result, farmland is
precious and in many
places great care is taken
with tiny patches of
ground to obtain the
largest yields possible.
Rice is the main crop in
much of Asia and whole
hillsides are sometimes
terraced to provide the
flooded paddyfields this
crop needs in order to
grow.

Left: Hong Kong, a minute
British colony off the
coast of China, is one of
the greatest trading
centres in Asia.

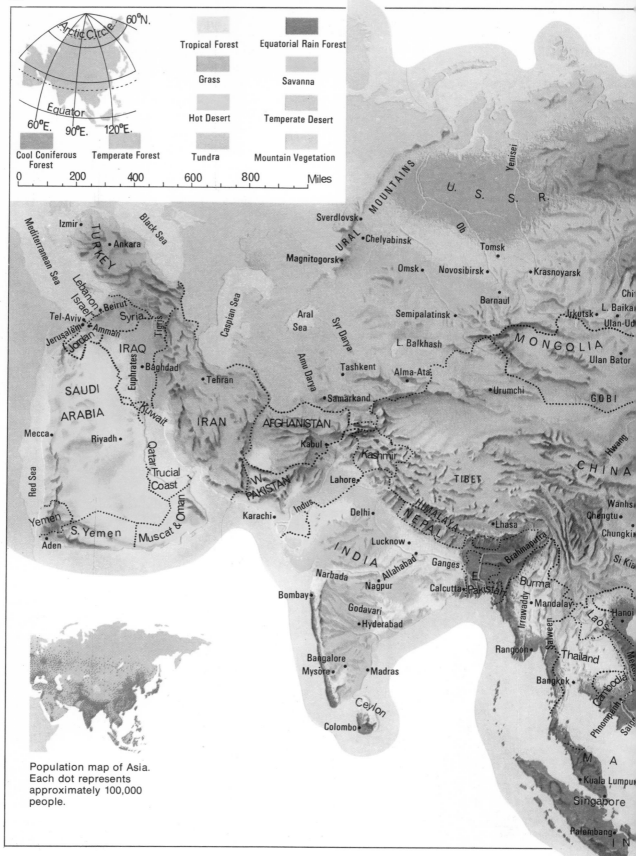

Tropical Forest

Equatorial Rain Forest

Grass

Savanna

Hot Desert

Temperate Desert

Cool Coniferous Forest

Temperate Forest

Tundra

Mountain Vegetation

60°N.

Arctic Circle

Equator

60°E. 90°E. 120°E.

0 200 400 600 800 Miles

Population map of Asia.
Each dot represents
approximately 100,000
people.

Izmir
Ankara
TURKEY
Black Sea
Mediterranean Sea
Lebanon
Israel
Beirut
Tel-Aviv
Jerusalem
Amman
Jordan
Syria
Tigris
IRAQ
Baghdad
Euphrates
SAUDI
ARABIA
Kuwait
Mecca
Riyadh
Qatar
Red Sea
Trucial
Coast
Yemen
S. Yemen
Aden
Muscat & Oman

Caspian Sea
Tehran
IRAN
Karachi

URAL MOUNTAINS
Sverdlovsk
Chelyabinsk
Magnitogorsk
Omsk
Aral
Sea
Syr Darya
Amu Darya
Tashkent
Samarkand
AFGHANISTAN
Kabul
Kashmir
W.
PAKISTAN
Lahore
Indus
Delhi

U. S. S. R.
Yenisei
Ob
Tomsk
Novosibirsk
Krasnoyarsk
Barnaul
Semipalatinsk
Irkutsk
Ulan-U
L. Baika
MONGOLIA
L. Balkhash
Alma-Ata
Urumchi
Ulan Bator
GOBI
TIBET
CHINA
Chi
Wanhs
Chengtu
Chungki
Si Kia
Lhasa
HIMALAYA
NEPAL
Lucknow
INDIA
Narbada
Allahabad
Nagpur
Ganges
Calcutta
E.
Pakistan
Brahmaputra
Burma
Mandalay
Hanoi
Laos
Irrawaddy
Salween
Meko
Bombay
Godavari
Hyderabad
Rangoon
Thailand
Bangalore
Mysore
Madras
Bangkok
Cambodia
Phnompenh
Saig
Ceylon
Colombo
MA
Kuala Lumpu
Singapore
Palembang
IN
Djakarta

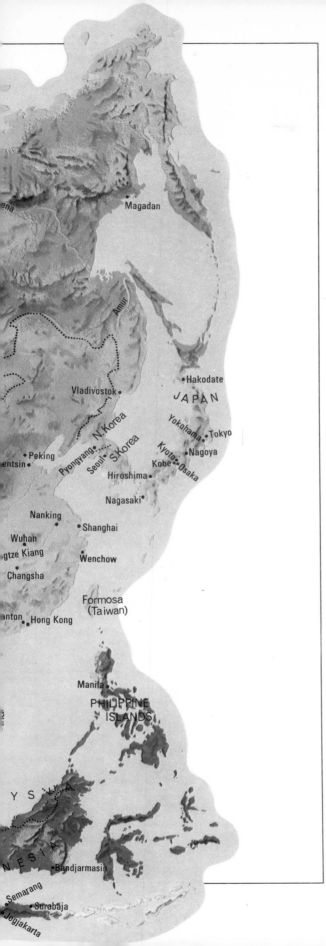

where nearly half the Asian people live.

Southern Asia is the region that lies to the south of the Himalaya mountains. It includes the ancient plateaus of Afghanistan, Bhutan, India and Pakistan. *Southwestern Asia* is a dry region that includes Turkey, Iran and the Arabian Peninsula. *South-eastern Asia* includes the land south of China and east of India, and the Indonesian, Malaysian and Philippine islands.

There are some large bodies of inland water in Asia. The Caspian Sea, the world's largest inland sea, lies between Asia and Europe. The shore of the Dead Sea, partly in Israel and partly in Jordan, lies about 1,300 feet below sea level.

Among many huge rivers in Asia the Lena, Yenisei, and Ob are frozen for part of their courses during six months of each year. In the spring, when the rivers are full, and their mouths are still ice-bound, great floods occur. Other important rivers are the Jordan, that flows southwards from Lebanon to the Dead Sea; the Tigris and Euphrates, which drain Iraq; the Brahmaputra and the Ganges that empty into the Bay of Bengal through a common delta; and the Indus, which rises in western Tibet and flows into the Arabian Sea.

In China the chief rivers are the Hwang, the Si-Kiang, and the Yangtze. The plain of Manchuria is drained by the Amur and its tributary, the Sungari. The mountains in or near Tibet give rise to several major rivers, among them the Brahmaputra, Hwang, Indus, Mekong, Salween and Yangtze.

Deserts are plentiful throughout Asia. Most of the Arabian Peninsula is desert, and the Gobi desert occupies an enormous plateau in central Asia.

The far north of Asia has an arctic climate, and the southern regions are equatorial. The interior of the continent suffers great extremes of climate. Winters are bitterly cold but summers produce a fierce heat. These extremes cause great differences in pressure and wind systems and are the cause of the violent *monsoons* (seasonal winds) that bring heavy rain to all of south-east Asia from May to October.

Asian wild animals include tigers, monkeys, rhinoceroses, bears, deer, mongooses, and many kinds of poisonous and non-poisonous snakes. Some wild animals, such as the elephant and the water buffalo, have been tamed and trained to work in the forests and fields.

Vegetation varies with the climate.

Northern Asia contains the world's largest fir and pine forest. Temperate grasslands and desert scrub cover some other parts of the continent.

Most people in Asia eat rice as their main food. Rice grows in the wet, tropical regions. In drier areas other cereals such as maize, wheat, millet and soya beans are grown. Timber is a valuable product. The tropical regions yield quantities of teak, pine wood comes from Siberia, and hardwoods from the forests of China.

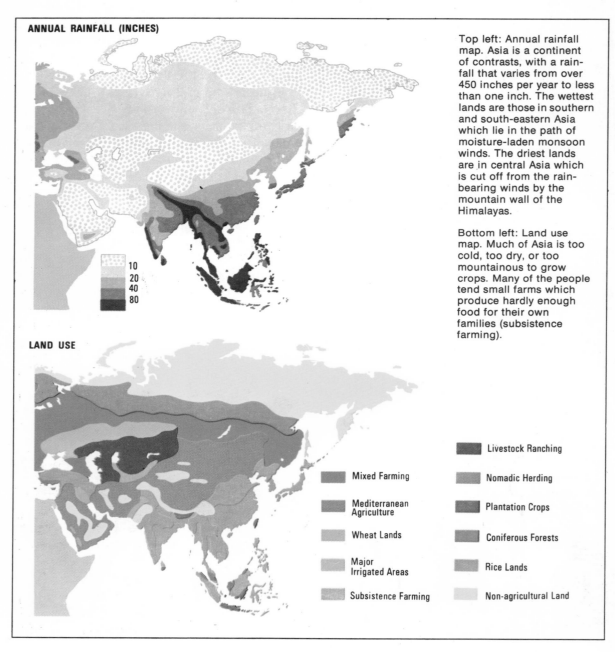

ANNUAL RAINFALL (INCHES)

10
20
40
80

LAND USE

Top left: Annual rainfall map. Asia is a continent of contrasts, with a rainfall that varies from over 450 inches per year to less than one inch. The wettest lands are those in southern and south-eastern Asia which lie in the path of moisture-laden monsoon winds. The driest lands are in central Asia which is cut off from the rain-bearing winds by the mountain wall of the Himalayas.

Bottom left: Land use map. Much of Asia is too cold, too dry, or too mountainous to grow crops. Many of the people tend small farms which produce hardly enough food for their own families (subsistence farming).

Mixed Farming

Mediterranean Agriculture

Wheat Lands

Major Irrigated Areas

Subsistence Farming

Livestock Ranching

Nomadic Herding

Plantation Crops

Coniferous Forests

Rice Lands

Non-agricultural Land

INDEPENDENT COUNTRIES OF ASIA

Country	Area (sq. mi.)	Population	Capital
Afghanistan	253,861	16,070,000	Kabul
Burma	261,789	25,016,000	Rangoon
Cambodia	69,898	6,484,000	Phnom Penh
Ceylon	25,332	11,678,000	Colombo
China	3,691,502	700,000,000	Peking
Cyprus	3,572	595,000	Nicosia
Formosa (Taiwan) [Nationalist China]	13,885	12,233,000	Taipei
India	1,262,274	489,254,000	New Delhi
Indonesia	735,269	106,777,000	Djakarta
Iran (Persia)	636,294	22,857,000	Tehran
Iraq	173,260	8,350,000	Baghdad
Israel	7,992	2,386,000	Jerusalem
Japan	142,726	97,913,000	Tokyo
Jordan	37,301	2,035,000	Amman
Korea, North	46,540	11,289,000	Pyongyang
Korea, South	38,004	29,095,000	Seoul
Kuwait	6,000	231,000	Kuwait
Laos	91,429	2,024,000	Vientiane
Lebanon	4,015	2,080,000	Beirut
Malaysia	128,654	11,561,000	Kuala Lumpur
Maldive Islands	115	93,000	Malé
Mongolia	592,665	1,091,000	Ulan Bator
Nepal	54,362	10,210,000	Katmandu
Pakistan	365,529	107,009,000	Islamabad
Philippines	115,707	32,926,000	Quezon City
Russia (Asiatic)	6,498,500	55,400,000	Moscow
Saudi Arabia	870,000	6,820,000	Riyadh
Singapore	224	2,007,000	Singapore
South Yemen	60,000	900,000	Aden
Syria	71,228	5,595,000	Damascus
Thailand (Siam)	194,456	31,647,000	Bangkok
Turkey (Asiatic)	292,260	29,683,000	Ankara
Vietnam, North	61,294	18,797,000	Hanoi
Vietnam, South	65,948	16,012,000	Saigon
Yemen	75,290	4,978,000	Sana

COLONIES AND TERRITORIES IN ASIA

Name	Area (sq.mi.)	Population	Capital	Status
Bahrein	231	151,000	Manama	British protected sheikdom
Bhutan	18,147	748,000	Thimbu	Monarchy under Indian protection
Brunei	2,226	102,000	Brunei	Sultanate under British protection
Hong Kong	398	3,810,000	Victoria	British crown colony
Macao	6	175,000	Macao	Portuguese colony
Muscat and Oman	82,000	697,000	Muscat	British protected sultanate
Portuguese Timor	5,763	571,000	Dili	Portuguese colony
Qatar	8,500	42,000	Doha	Sheikdom under British protection
Ryukyu Islands (Southern)	848	968,000	Naha	Japanese islands under U.S. military administration
Sikkim	2,744	177,000	Gangtok	Monarchy under Indian protection
Trucial States	32,278	111,000	Dubai	Seven sheikdoms under British protection

Farmland in Asia is often too precious for growing crops to be used for rearing animals. Consequently, fishing is important in coastal regions.

A Buddhist temple in Bangkok. Temples account for one-quarter of the city area. Asia was the birthplace of all the world's great religions.

Temperature maps of Asia for January and July.

January

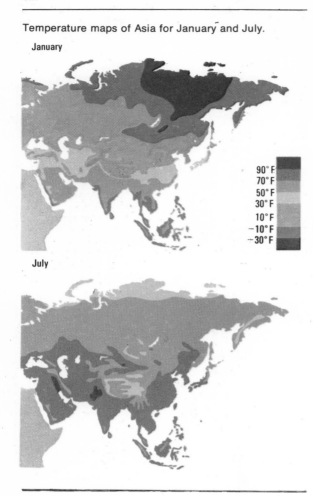

90°F
70°F
50°F
30°F
10°F
−10°F
−30°F

July

Other important agricultural products are tea, tobacco, rubber, dates, jute, cotton and olives.

Much Asian industry consists of handicrafts produced in small factories and workshops. The great exception is Japan. Japan leads the world in shipbuilding and is also a leading steel producer. Northern China, parts of India, and central Siberia also have modern, well-equipped factories that produce a wide range of goods. But most Asian nations export few manufactured goods because they are unable to meet the needs of their own people. Many exports are minerals. A quarter of the world's petroleum comes from southeastern and south-western Asia. Turkey and the Philippines export chromite, and nearly two-thirds of the world's tin comes from south-eastern Asia.

Most of the world's earliest civilizations and all the world's great religions began in Asia. More than 2,000 years ago powerful empires flourished in the continent. Their peoples reached a high development in the arts and sciences. They began to influence Europe, especially through contact with the ancient Greeks, from about 300 B.C. But because the various Asian peoples were separated from each other by vast deserts and lofty mountain ranges, they never became as closely knit as some of their western neighbours. They gradually developed different languages, customs and ways of life.

After World War II the political map of Asia was profoundly altered. Many nations once subject to colonial rule achieved their independence.

Assassins During the eleventh century a Persian called Hasan founded a Mohammedan religious Order. They were mystics and took drugs, and they murdered their enemies. The Order was tightly disciplined. In 1090 Hasan made his headquarters in Khorassan in a castle called Alamut, which meant the Eagle's Nest. Hasan and his successors were called Sheikh-el-Jebel, the 'Old Man of the Mountains' to Europeans. Hasan's followers were called Hashshashin, hashish-eaters, which became Assassins in English. Assassination means murdering for religious or political reasons.

The Assassins had an active headquarters in Syria and many secret branches. They were opposed to the religious views of most rulers of the Mohammedan world. For 150 years they terrorized the Middle East with religious and political murders. Even Saladin was unable to destroy them. They often allied with the European Crusaders against their fellow religionists. Only in 1255 was their power ended and the Order of Assassins almost wiped out by the Mongols. Their example has been copied ever since by groups of fanatics, with tragic results for many famous men.

Assyrians The Assyrians were a Semitic people living in the north of Mesopotamia. Their chief city was Assur. They were merchants and soldiers. First they threw off Sumerian rule (see Sumer) and then between 1726-1694 B.C., they conquered neighbouring tribes and built up an empire. But it was short lived. Assyria became a subject state of Babylonia (see Babylonia) after 1679 B.C. and did not begin to expand again for many centuries.

Under Tiglath-Pileser I, the Assyrians began to conquer other tribes again and in 1097 B.C. they sacked Babylon. Tiglath-Pileser's successors, in spite of many revolts by the people they conquered, pushed the frontiers of the Assyrian empire as far as Egypt. In 673 B.C. King Esarhaddon launched a successful attack on Egypt and brought it under his control. During the reign of his son Ashurbanipal (669-626 B.C.) Assyria's empire reached its greatest extent. Then, it collapsed even more swiftly than it had risen. The Babylonians first broke away from Assyrian rule in 626 B.C. and in 612 B.C., in alliance with the Chaldeans, they captured Nine-

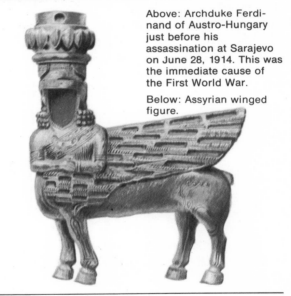

Above: Archduke Ferdinand of Austro-Hungary just before his assassination at Sarajevo on June 28, 1914. This was the immediate cause of the First World War.

Below: Assyrian winged figure.

veh. In 610 B.C. an Egyptian army arrived too late to save Harran, the last Assyrian city to be subdued.

The Assyrian empire was above all a military one. They were a nation of warriors and the king's main task was to lead the army. The officers were Assyrians, but the ordinary soldiers were mercenaries (men who were paid to fight) drawn from the various tribes within the empire. They

fought in war chariots and on foot and they had skilled engineers to conduct sieges. The ruins of the splendid temples and palaces which the Kings of Assyria built are covered with sculptures and bas reliefs (raised pictures cut in stone) showing incidents from their battles. Ashurbanipal's library has also been preserved, so providing written records of the empire.

Two great weaknesses that seem to have helped to bring down the empire were its failure to make Assyrian rule popular with the conquered peoples and the extravagant sums spent on building.

Asteroids are small planets whose paths around the Sun lie mainly between those of Mars and Jupiter. About 2,000 of them have been found. Only one, Vesta, can be seen with the naked eye, and even then only on the clearest nights. The largest asteroid, Ceres, is only 480 miles across. Some astronomers believe that the asteroids may be the remains of a planet which broke up long ago.

Astrology Many newspapers and magazines contain columns called something like "What the Stars Foretell" written by *astrologers*. Astrology is the study of the Sun, Moon, planets, and stars to find out how they influence people and their affairs. It is quite different from *astronomy*. Astronomers do not believe that astrology is a science at all. They cannot see how lumps of matter, millions of miles away in space, can possibly affect the lives of men and women.

The astrologer *casts a horoscope* for a person. He draws a diagram showing the position of the heavenly bodies and the 12 signs of the zodiac at the time of the person's birth. From this he claims to be able to describe that person's character and foretell the main events of his future.

For thousands of years astrologers were among the most important people in the courts of kings. They used the stars to interpret dreams and unusual events and to foretell the future. Their early studies paved the way for modern astronomy.

Above: Ceres, the largest asteroid, compared in size with the British Isles.

Right: Astrologers believed the signs of the zodiac ruled various parts of the body.

Astronautics is the branch of science which deals with the many problems of space flight.

The Space Age began with the launching of the artificial satellite Sputnik 1 on October 4, 1957. Less than four years later, on April 12, 1961, came the first manned flight. The Russian Yuri Gagarin made one orbit of the Earth in his spacecraft Vostok 1. He was the first spacepilot, or *astronaut*. (The Russian term is *cosmonaut*.) Since then, astronauts have journeyed millions of miles in space in preparation for a Moon landing. The American Moon project is called Apollo.

Most manned and unmanned spacecraft have been artificial satellites of the Earth, travelling round and round the Earth in orbit (see Satellites).

A spacecraft is carried into orbit on top of a massive rocket, which lifts it clear of the Earth's atmosphere and gives it the very high speed required to keep it in orbit (see Rocket).

A spacecraft can stay in orbit if it has enough speed to overcome the 'pull' of the Earth, or *gravity*. For an orbit 100 miles above the Earth, this *orbital velocity* is about 17,500 miles an hour. At this distance and orbital velocity the tendency of the spacecraft to fly away from the Earth (like a stone from a sling) is balanced by the pull of gravity.

There is, then, no effective gravity in orbit. Everything is therefore weightless. This state is often called zero G, G standing for gravity.

The spacecraft must be lifted above the Earth's atmosphere to avoid the resistance, or *drag*, of the air. Drag would quickly slow it down and make it fall back to Earth. Also friction with the air would heat the craft and might even make it burn up, just like a meteor does.

Launching an astronaut into space and bringing him back is a very hazardous business. To start with, he has to withstand the great forces of acceleration during take-off. Then he must adjust to the effects of weightlessness in orbit. He must

be protected by his spacecraft or a spacesuit from the cold and airless world of space. Finally, he must return from orbit and survive the rapid slowing down and heating effects caused by the drag of the atmosphere.

Astronauts receive special training to prepare themselves for space flights. For example, they spend a long time in a machine called a centrifuge, which whirls them round and round rapidly and reproduces the kind of forces they can expect during take-off and landing.

The astronauts also train in dummy spacecraft which can be made to do many of the things a real one does in space.

After months of intensive training, the astronauts climb into their spacecraft and are rocketed into space. They lie on their backs during launching because this is the best way to withstand the great 'push' of the rocket.

Up in orbit the astronauts, like everything else, are weightless. Nothing keeps them 'down', and they can float around freely. Eating and drinking are very different from on Earth. Food and drink must be squeezed right into the mouth.

The crew cabin of the spacecraft is connected to what is known as a *life-support system*. This provides gas under pressure for the astronauts to breathe, removes stale air and moisture, and keeps the temperature steady.

Returning to Earth is probably the most dangerous part of the space flight. To fall down from orbit, the spacecraft must be slowed down to below orbital velocity. This is done by firing rockets called *retro-rockets* in the direction in which the spacecraft is travelling.

After the retro-rockets have fired, the capsule containing the astronauts separates from the rest of the craft. It drops rapidly towards the Earth and re-enters the atmosphere. The atmosphere acts like a brake and quickly slows down the capsule and heats it at the same time. The base of the capsule glows red-hot, but it is specially designed as a *heat*

Above: The problem of the tremendous thrust required for a space-launch was solved by building multi-stage rockets. When the first stage burns out it falls away, leaving the progressively smaller second and third stages less weight to propel upwards.

Top right: Man 'walks' in space. Travelling at the same speed as the spacecraft to which he is attached, the astronaut is weightless.

Middle right: American astronauts land in the sea. The space capsule floats, but frogmen attach a buoyant collar around it as a precaution.

Bottom right: An astronaut's full space-rig is airtight. On the ground a portable air-conditioner is attached to it.

shield to protect the astronauts inside. As the capsule falls lower, parachutes open and gently lower it to the ground or the sea.

Astronomy is the scientific study of the stars, planets, and other heavenly bodies. For many thousands of years men have watched the skies and tried to explain what they have seen there. The movements of the Sun, the Moon, and some stars were used by early Man as a calendar to guide him in planting and reaping his crops.

The astronomer, like any other scientist, needs a laboratory and instruments. His 'laboratory' is called an *observatory*. His most important instrument is the *telescope*. Most observatories are equipped with various kinds of telescopes.

Powerful telescopes are required because the astronomer is studying objects so far away that their distances are measured not in miles but in *light-years*. One light-year is the distance travelled by a ray of light in one year; it is nearly six million million (6,000,000,000,000) miles.

Some people study the stars and planets as a hobby. Many important discoveries have been made by amateur astronomers using small telescopes.

Athens is the capital and largest city of Greece. It is the seat of the Greek government and the commercial centre of the Attica region. For centuries it has been a centre of Greek learning and art.

The city is situated on the plain of Attica close to the southern tip of the Greek mainland. Piraeus, the city's seaport, is six miles from the centre on the Apollo coast of the Saronic Gulf. The ancient city first clustered around the Acropolis rock, but modern development has spread far out to the slopes of the surrounding mountains. The total urban population now numbers over 1,850,000.

The ruined temples and statues of the Acropolis, topped by the Parthenon, and

The Parthenon is the most famous of the many monuments to Athens' glorious past which attract countless visitors to the city.

many little Byzantine churches, provide strange contrast with the Royal Palace, university, and modern office buildings. By virtue of its history and monuments, the city attracts thousands of visitors.

Athletics Track and Field Athletics originated in Greece about the 9th century B.C. with the running, jumping and throwing events of the Ancient Olympic Games. These events were revived in the English universities in the mid-19th century. The Amateur Athletic Association was formed in 1880. The revival of the Olympic Games in 1896 awakened worldwide interest in the sport.

Track events are running races on the flat, or over obstacles, over recognised distances from 100 yards to 6 miles or more. World records are measured in both yards and metres (100 metres = 109 yards 1 foot, 1 inch). Field events normally include the high jump, pole vault, long jump, triple jump, shot putt, and the discus, hammer and javelin throws.

Races up to and including 400 metres (or 440 yards) are run in lanes to allow a separate course for each competitor. Starting blocks are permitted for sprint races. Races start with warning commands, then a pistol shot. A competitor may be disqualified for deliberately impeding another's progress.

The finish is a line drawn across the track at right angles to the inner edge, and a runner is placed according to when his chest reaches the line. The tape is merely a guide for the judges.

High jumpers and pole vaulters attempt to clear a cross-bar set at a starting height decided by the judges or laid down by the organizers. Three consecutive failures mean disqualification. For each succeeding round the height of the bar is raised. For the vault, a pole of any material, length or diameter may be used. Just

before take-off its base is 'planted' in a specially provided box.

The long jumper is allowed an unlimited run-up, but must take-off from a white wooden take-off board, 4 feet long, into a landing area. Each jump is measured from a scratch line made at the end of the board to the nearest break made in the sand of the landing area. The triple jump consists of a hop, a step, then a long jump.

The Marathon is a road race of exactly 26 miles 385 yards and usually commences and finishes at a stadium. The Decathlon comprises ten events in the following order: 100 metres, long jump, shot, high jump, 400 metres, 110 metres hurdles, discus, pole vault, javelin, 1,500 metres.

The shot and hammer, and discus are thrown from a special circle, 7 feet in diameter for the shot and hammer, 8 feet 2¼ inches for the discus. The shot is a solid iron (or other metal) ball weighing 16 pounds minimum (7.257 kilograms). The discus is made of wood or plastic,

Hurdling

Throwing the Discus

with a smooth metal rim, its minimum weight being 4 pounds 6½ ounces (2 kilograms), diameter 8⅝ inches. The hammer is a metal sphere attached to a length of spring steel wire, its complete minimum weight being 16 pounds.

The time of 10 seconds for 100 yards was first bettered on October 11, 1890 by John Owen in the U.S.A. Championships at Washington, but in 1969 the world record stood at 9.1 seconds. The first high jump of over 6 feet was made on March 17, 1876 by Marshall James Brooks at Marston, near Oxford. The record in 1969 was 7 feet 5¾ inches. Dr. Roger Bannister, C.B.E., of England, was first to run one mile in under 4 minutes. His time on May 6, 1954 at Iffley Road, Oxford, was 3 minutes 59.4 seconds.

America has produced most of the world's outstanding athletes. Among them is Jesse Owens who won gold medals in the 100 and 200 metres, the long jump and the 4 × 100 metres relay at the 1936 Olympic games in Berlin.

Atlantic Ocean is the sea lying between Europe and Africa in the east, and the Americas in the west. It is the second largest body of water in the world, after the Pacific Ocean, and covers about a sixth of the Earth's surface. It has an area of 31,530,000 square miles, and an average depth of more than 6,000 feet. The Equator divides the ocean into the North and South Atlantic.

It was named *Atlantic* after the Atlas mountains in north-western Africa. The ocean lay beyond the mountains and was alleged to surround a legendary continent or island called *Atlantis*.

Although the Atlantic has eastern and western boundaries, it has no definite northern and southern limits, because it merges with the Arctic and Antarctic Oceans, respectively. Measured from the Arctic Circle to the Antarctic Circle, the Atlantic is about 9,000 miles long. At its widest point, it is 5,000 miles across.

A number of important islands lie in the Atlantic. Among these are the British

Pole Vault

Long Jump

Sprint

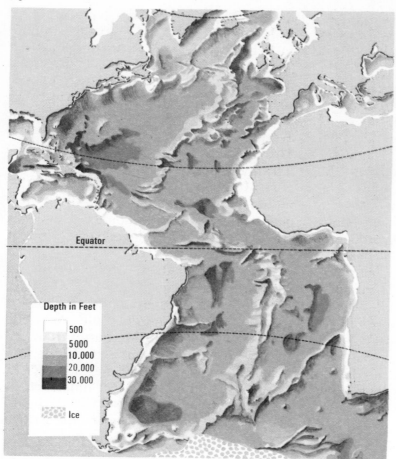

Equator

Depth in Feet

500
5000
10,000
20,000
30,000

Ice

Isles, Newfoundland, Greenland, Iceland, the West Indies, the Azores, the Canary Islands and the Cape Verde Islands. Large, open coastal waters lead off both sides of the Atlantic. These include the Gulf of Guinea, the Bay of Biscay and the North Sea on the eastern side; and Hudson Bay, the Gulf of St Lawrence, the Gulf of Mexico and the Caribbean Sea on the western side. Major semi-enclosed seas in the east include the Mediterranean and the Baltic.

The bottom of the Atlantic is divided into two deep valleys either side of a twisted ridge, the *mid-Atlantic Ridge*, that runs from north to south down the middle of the ocean. It lies at an average depth of about 10,000 feet below the water's surface, but occasionally juts above the surface in the form of islands, such as Iceland, the Azores and Tristan da Cunha.

There are a number of strong currents in the Atlantic. Perhaps the best known of these is the Gulf Stream. This current carries warm water across the North Atlantic from the Gulf of Mexico north-eastwards towards the coasts of Europe. It keeps western Europe comparatively warm and ice-free in the winter months. The Labrador Current, on the other hand, brings icy water from the Arctic down the eastern coasts of North America, and sometimes carries icebergs that are a danger to shipping.

There are several parts of Atlantic coastal waters that are particularly rich in fish. Such places are the Grand Banks off Newfoundland, and the Dogger Bank in the North Sea.

Water temperature in the ocean deeps is always near freezing point, but at the surface it varies from about 80° F in the tropics to 28° F near the Arctic and Antarctic circles.

Atmosphere The entire surface of the Earth is covered by an immense 'sea' of air, stretching upwards to a height of several hundred miles. This covering of air is known as the *atmosphere*. It is usually thought of as consisting of three layers: the *troposphere*, which stretches from sea level to between 5 and 10 miles up; the *stratosphere*, which extends from between 5 and 10 miles up to 50 miles up; and the *ionosphere*, which lies beyond.

The air becomes 'thinned-out' as we move away from the Earth's surface. The oxygen that air contains is essential to all living creatures, so that man cannot survive at any great height without some kind of mechanical aid. Even at heights of three miles or less, the thinning-out of the air is very noticeable, causing an uncomfortable shortness of breath. For this reason, mountaineers, especially when climbing the highest peaks, such as Mount Everest, are often forced to use oxygen masks.

Life as we know it is possible because our Earth has an atmosphere. To appreciate the importance of the atmosphere, consider the Moon, which has no atmosphere. Temperatures in the daytime are so high that if the Moon had any water it would boil. And at night it is very much colder even than the coldest places on Earth. But on Earth the atmosphere acts as a shield during the day, protecting us from the Sun's rays, and as a blanket at night, holding the heat in.

We do not usually think of air as having weight, but in fact it has. The total weight of the atmosphere is nearly 6,000 million million tons. The column of air rising above each of us weighs about a ton and exerts a pressure of about 15 pounds on every square inch at sea level. We do not notice this tremendous pressure because the pressure inside our bodies is the same as that outside, just as the pressure inside deep-sea crea-

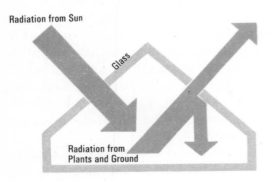

Right: Temperatures in the atmosphere.

Top left: The upper levels of the atmosphere are vital to long-distance radio communications because they reflect radio waves back to the ground, allowing them to travel around the Earth's curved surface. The Heaviside Layer reflects longer wavelengths, the Appleton Layer reflects shorter wavelengths. Very short wavelengths pass straight on into space, but they are sometimes reflected by meteor streams.

Bottom left: By letting through most of the Sun's radiation, but trapping much of the Earth's longer wavelength radiation, the atmosphere acts as a greenhouse over the Earth, keeping the temperature higher beneath it than above it.

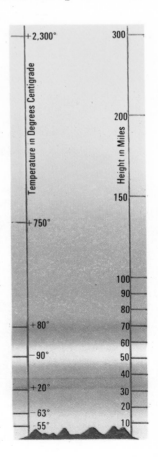

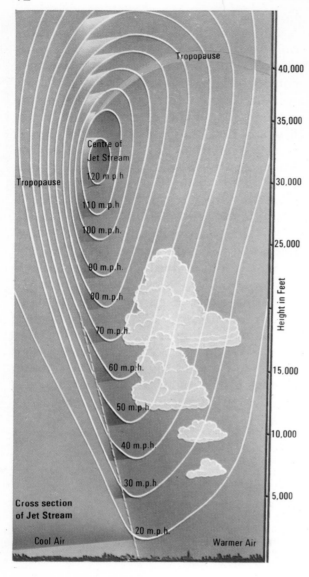

Above: A jet stream is a channel of quickly-moving air occurring at about 30,000 feet. At its centre, air is travelling at between 100 and 200 miles per hour.

Below: The composition of air.

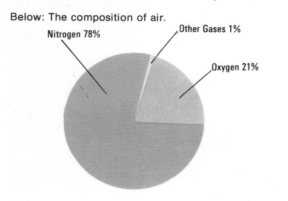

tures is the same as the tremendous pressure of the surrounding water.

The higher we go in the atmosphere, the lower the pressure, because there is less air above us and, as a result, less weight of air. Thirty miles up, the air pressure is only one-thousandth of the air pressure at sea level.

Conditions in the troposphere, the lowest layer of the atmosphere, create the world's weather. In the troposphere, temperatures usually decrease with height at the rate of 3·5° F for every thousand feet (6° C for every thousand metres). But at the boundary between the troposphere and the stratosphere above, the temperature stops falling for a while. This is called the *tropopause*. In certain places along the tropopause there are winds of over 100 miles per hour. These are called *jet streams*.

The stratosphere is generally much calmer than the troposphere and is used by high-flying aircraft to avoid bad weather conditions.

The outermost layer of the atmosphere, the ionosphere, is important in long-range radio communications. It reflects medium and long radio waves back to the ground, making it possible for them to travel around the Earth's curved surface.

Atom Everything in the universe is made of incredibly tiny particles called atoms. Atoms are so small that if ten thousand million could be placed end to end they would measure half an inch. An atom is like a solar system in miniature. It has a central 'sun' or *nucleus* which has a number of 'planets' or *electrons* 'orbiting' around it. The nucleus itself is made of two kinds of particles: *protons* (which are electrically positive) and *neutrons*, so-called because they are electrically neutral. The orbiting electrons are electrically negative.

Different elements are made of different atoms, the difference being in the number of orbiting electrons (called the

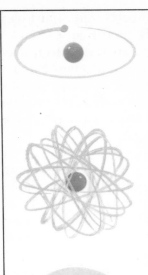

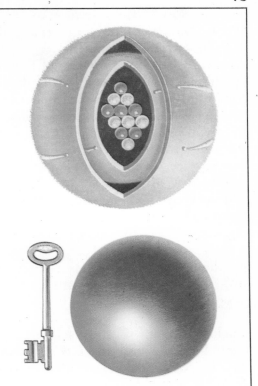

Top left: A hydrogen atom consists of a single electron moving round a single proton, like a planet in orbit round the Sun.

Middle left: The orbit changes its position so rapidly that it seems to weave a solid shell round the nucleus.

Bottom left: Here the orbit is shown as a shell, but cut away to reveal the proton at the centre.

Top right: A carbon atom contains six protons and six neutrons in its nucleus. Six electrons circle the nucleus, two in an inner shell and four in an outer shell.

Bottom right: Atoms are so incredibly small that if the key was enlarged until it stretched 25,000 miles around the Earth each atom in the key would still be no larger than this red ball.

atomic number) and the number of protons plus neutrons in the nucleus (called the *mass number*).

The word 'atom' comes from the Greek *atomos* meaning 'that which cannot be divided'. More than 2,000 years ago the Greek philosopher Democritus suggested that if something was halved, then halved again, and again, then eventually there would be tiny pieces which could never be any smaller. Today, of course, we know that the atom is made of smaller particles.

Ninety-two different atoms (and therefore elements) exist in nature. Others have been made artificially in the laboratory. Scientists list atoms in order of atomic number in the *periodic table*.

Like our solar system, atoms are mostly space. In 1919 Lord Rutherford bombarded gold foil with particles emitted from a piece of radium and found that most of them passed straight through. Rutherford also concluded that practically all of the atom's mass is concentrated in its nucleus.

In an element atoms are held together by mutual attraction. In a *solid* this attraction is strong. In a *liquid* it is weak. In a *gas* the atoms move freely. Heating can weaken the attraction between atoms, thus changing an element from a solid to a liquid, and then to a gas.

Attila (about A.D. 406-453). In the fifth century, civilization had developed to a high degree in western Europe under the dominion of the Roman Empire. But in eastern Europe there were wandering, warlike tribes whom the Romans called *barbarians*. The Huns, one of the largest barbarian tribes, were led by Attila.

The Huns were not a united people. They lived in scattered groups, moving from place to place. The centre of Attila's kingdom was Hungary. From there he gathered the Huns together into a large army and conquered the tribes in the territory surrounding his. Eventually almost all of eastern Europe was under his control.

Threatening to attack the Roman Empire, he forced the emperor to pay him a yearly tribute to prevent attack. But he still looted towns on the edges of the empire. After several years of this uneasy relationship with Rome, Attila demanded the emperor's sister in marriage. He also required that a quarter of the empire be given to him as her inheritance. When the emperor refused, Attila stormed into the empire. But the Roman army forced him to retreat.

Two years later he invaded the empire again. He ravaged many cities before disease among his troops forced him to retreat once more. The following year he died, and without his strong leadership the Huns again became a scattered people.

Auckland, a prosperous seaport and the capital of Auckland province, is the largest city in New Zealand. With a population of 579,000 it is beautifully set astride the Tamaki Isthmus, a narrow neck of land on North Island. The city is important as a manufacturing centre, with clothing, footwear and engineering industries. There are two harbours. Nearby rich farming land contributes to the port's prosperity. There are Anglican and Roman Catholic cathedrals and a university. The War Memorial Museum has a unique collection of Maori relics and carvings.

Aurora is a beautiful display of lights in the upper atmosphere caused by particles shot out from the Sun. The aurora (plural *aurorae*) seen in the night sky of the northern hemisphere is called *aurora borealis,* or *northern lights.* A similar display seen in the southern hemisphere is called *aurora australis,* or *southern lights.*

Aurorae are present all the time in most parts of the sky, but can be seen clearly with the unaided eye only in the extreme north and south.

The electrically charged particles from the Sun that cause the aurorae are deflected towards the polar regions by the Earth's magnetism. The particles collide with particles in the gases of the Earth's atmosphere, causing patterns of brilliant glowing lights. The main colours are green and red. Aurorae nearly always occur more than 50 miles above the Earth's surface, and are sometimes more than 500 miles high.

Australia is a country that is also a continent. It lies in the southern hemisphere. It is about three-quarters of the size of Europe, but Europe has 56 times as many people. Australia is a member of the Commonwealth of Nations.

Several islands lie around the coast. The largest and most important of these is Tasmania, which is south of the mainland of Australia. The Great Barrier Reef on the north-eastern coast is a 1,200-mile chain of coral reefs and islets.

Most of the western and central part of Australia is a high, flat plateau. Few people live there. The eastern third of the continent is more varied. Close to the east coast is a long range of mountains, called the Great Dividing Range. The highest mountain is Mount Kosciusko (7,316 feet).

The northern part of Australia lies in the tropics, just north of the Tropic of Capricorn. Along the coast, it is hot and wet, with heavy rains every year. South-eastern and south-western Australia have climates similar to those of California and the French Mediterranean coast, with hot, dry summers and warm, moist winters. The east coast also has sufficient rainfall for farming.

Most of the centre of the country has very unreliable rainfall. In some years, rain may fall, but several years of drought may follow.

Australia is rich in minerals, including bauxite, coal, copper, gold, iron, lead, nickel, silver, tin, uranium and zinc. Petroleum and natural gas have been found off the coasts. Huge underground stores of water lie under parts of the country called Artesian Basins.

Forests, particularly in the south and east, contain eucalyptus trees, which provide timber and oils. Australians call them gum trees.

Australia has only a few kinds of animals of its own. They include *marsupials,* which are animals with pouches. The biggest are the kangaroos. Others are koalas, wallabies and wombats. The duck-billed platypus, a mammal which lays eggs, is another Australian animal.

Most of the people of Australia are of British origin. Since World War II more than two million people from Europe have emigrated to Australia. In addition, there are about 40,000 Aborigines, a dark-skinned people whose ancestors were the first inhabitants of Australia.

More than half the people of Australia live in cities. The rest live in small towns or villages, or in lonely farms called *stations.* Some stations are many miles

Above: Australia is the stronghold of the marsupials—the pouched mammals. The young of marsupials are born in a relatively unformed state and continue their development in their mothers' pouch.

Top left: Ayers Rock, a famous landmark of Central Australia.

Bottom left: Harvest in New South Wales. The main wheat-growing areas are the Murray-Darling plains and the south-western corner of Western Australia. Australia exports large quantities of wheat.

Below: Australia has 164 million sheep, and accounts for almost half the world's wool exports.

ANNUAL RAINFALL (INCHES)

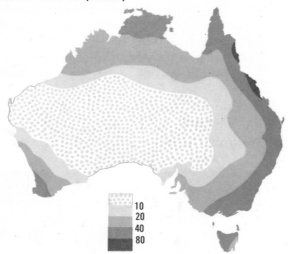

10
20
40
80

Annual rainfall map of Australia. The continent suffers from having its greatest width in the trade wind belt. These winds are being warmed as they blow towards the Equator and tend to pick up moisture rather than shed it. Only the two corners of Australia reach far enough south to catch rain from the wet westerly winds in winter.

LAND USE

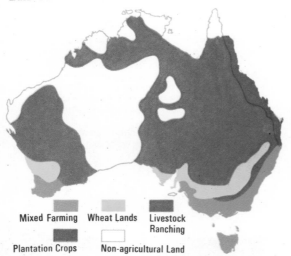

Mixed Farming   Wheat Lands   Livestock Ranching

Plantation Crops   Non-agricultural Land

Land use map of Australia. A considerable part of the continent is too dry for cattle or sheep ranching, and other areas are subject to irregular droughts.

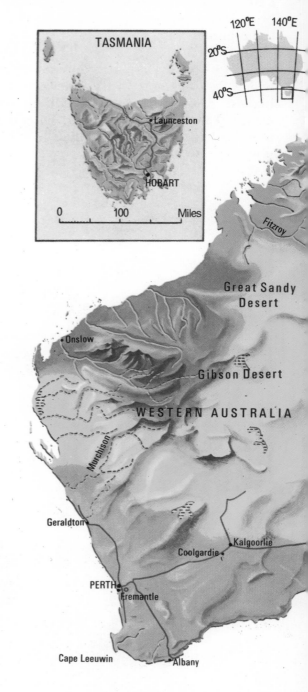

Chief Airports ⊙

Railways _____

Boundaries ____

Temperate Forest   Tropical Forest   Rain Forest   Grassland   Savanna   Hot Desert

0   200   400   600   Miles

Darwin

Gulf of Carpentaria

Cape York

Cooktown

NORTHERN TERRITORY

Forsayth

Townsville

Tennant Creek

Cloncurry

QUEENSLAND

Great Dividing Range

Alice Springs

Quilpie

Oodnadatta

Ipswich BRISBANE

Lake Eyre

Great Victoria
Desert

SOUTH AUSTRALIA

Bourke

Darling

Woomera

Broken Hill

NEW SOUTH WALES

Port Augusta

Great Australian Bight

Lachlan

NEWCASTLE

Murray

SYDNEY

Murrumbidgee

Wollongong

ADELAIDE

CANBERRA

VICTORIA

Bendigo

Cape Howe

Ballarat

Geelong

MELBOURNE

Bass Strait

Facts and Figures
Area: 2,967,741 square miles.
Population: 12,030,820.
Capital: Canberra.
Money Unit: Australian dollar.
Labour Force: 82% urban; 18% rural.
Exports: gold, meat, wheat, wool.
Imports: chemicals, machinery, vehicles.

STATES AND TERRITORIES OF AUSTRALIA

State or Territory	Area (sq. mi.)	Population	Capital
Australian Capital Territory	939	103,573	Canberra
New South Wales	309,433	4,300,083	Sydney
Northern Territory	520,280	39,556	Darwin
Queensland	667,000	1,688,529	Brisbane
South Australia	380,070	1,107,178	Adelaide
Tasmania	26,383	376,212	Hobart
Victoria	87,884	3,271,993	Melbourne
Western Australia	975,920	863,744	Perth

from other farms, and the people use radios and aircraft to keep in touch.

Mining and manufacturing provide more than two-thirds of Australia's wealth. The rest is provided by farming. The country exports great quantities of wool and wheat. It also has many cattle and produces much butter and cheese.

Australia has a federal form of government. This means that it is a *federation* or group of separate states, with a central government linking them together. Australia has six states: New South Wales, Queensland, South Australia, Tasmania, Victoria and Western Australia. Each state has its own parliament.

Two areas called territories come under the direct rule of the central government. They are the Northern Territory, much of which is desert, and the Australian Capital Territory, a small area around Canberra, the federal capital.

The first people to occupy Australia

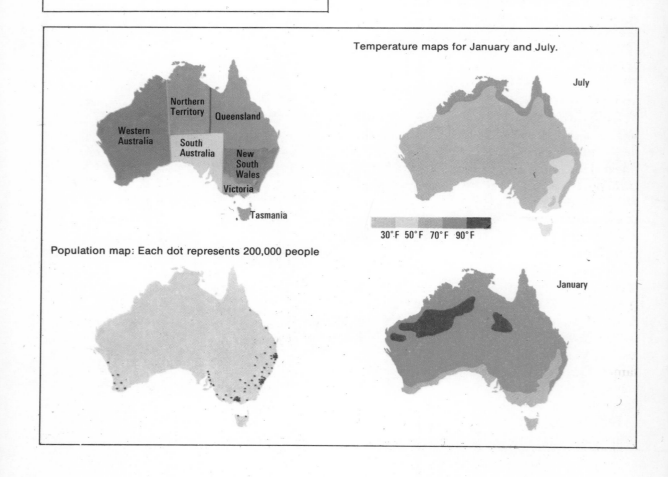

Temperature maps for January and July.

Population map: Each dot represents 200,000 people

30°F 50°F 70°F 90°F

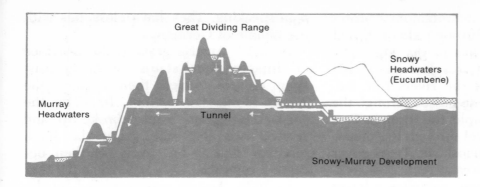

Left: A diagram of part of the Snowy Mountains scheme, one of the boldest irrigation and power projects of modern times. The abundant waters of the Snowy River are being impounded and led back through the mountains for electric power generation and to augment the Murray and Murrumbidgee rivers for inland irrigation.

were the Aborigines. They arrived in the continent about 20,000 years ago.

Australia was visited by Dutch explorers such as Tasman in the early 17th century, and at first it was called New Holland. Then, in 1770 the British explorer Captain James Cook landed in Botany Bay, on the south-eastern coast, and claimed the great unknown land for Britain.

The British decided to use the new territory as a *penal settlement*—a kind of open prison where criminals could be sent, guarded by a few soldiers. In 1788, 750 convicts and their escort arrived to set up a colony at Sydney, in the south-eastern part of Australia. During the next 70 years, a steady stream of people arrived in Australia to settle.

Gold was discovered in New South Wales and Victoria in 1851. During the next ten years about 700,000 people flocked to Australia to look for gold. The transportation of convicts had ceased by 1852, except to Western Australia, where it continued until 1867. Australia became an independent country in 1901 as the *Commonwealth of Australia.*

During World War I, Australian troops fought in Europe against the Germans as part of the Australian and New Zealand Army Corps (the Anzacs). Their bravery in attacking Germany's allies, the Turks, at Gallipoli in 1915 won them undying fame. During World War II, Australian forces fought in northern Africa and against the Japanese in New Guinea.

Before and after World War II, Australia grew both in population and wealth.

Top picture: Mining bauxite in the Darling Ranges near Perth, Western Australia. Australia possesses a plentiful supply of minerals.

Bottom picture: The 'flying doctor' is a famous Australian institution. In the remote areas known as the Outback people may live many miles from their nearest neighbour and hundreds of miles from the nearest hospital. Radio communication provides a link with neighbours and essential services.

More and more gold, wool and other Australian products were sold to other countries, and more people came to settle there. In 1965, Australian troops went to fight in the Vietnam war.